Fearless Pharaoh FooFoo
and
Other Dramas for Children

By Larry Vogel

CPH
SAINT LOUIS

Copyright © 1998 Concordia Publishing House
3558 S. Jefferson Avenue, St. Louis, MO 63118-3968
Manufactured in the United States of America

Library of Congress Cataloging–in–Publication Data

Vogel, Larry, 1953-
    Fearless Pharaoh foofoo and other dramas for children / by Larry Vogel.
        p.   cm.
    Includes index.
    ISBN 0-570-05332-3
       1. Bible—History of Biblical events—Juvenile drama.   2. Children's plays, American.
I. Title.
PS3572.02935F42   1998
812'.54—dc21   98-28472
                                                    CIP

1 2 3   4 5 6 7 8 9 10   07 06 05 04 03 02 01 00 99 98

Contents

With love and thanksgiving
for Betsy, Jessie, Michael, and Minka.

〰〰〰〰〰〰〰〰〰〰〰

Stage Direction Chart

UPSTAGE

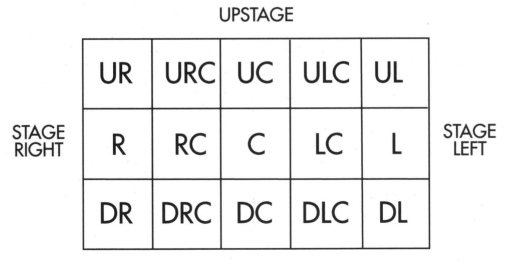

STAGE RIGHT

UR	URC	UC	ULC	UL
R	RC	C	LC	L
DR	DRC	DC	DLC	DL

STAGE LEFT

DOWNSTAGE

AUDIENCE

Introduction

The light-hearted dramas in this book were written for children—to help children learn the stories of the Bible from Genesis to the New Testament. The dramas can be used in school chapels, Sunday schools, camps, vacation Bible schools, or any other setting where children are learning about the Bible. The underlying theme is the sadness of sin and the wonder of God's sustaining love.

Students who have performed these dramas have enjoyed portraying a Bible-based story and getting a sense of understanding of the events Scripture describes. Students who have seen the dramas have demonstrated a greater understanding of the Bible events and a deeper sense of God's love in their lives. With a simple look at single events, each drama helps kids get a clearer picture of God's biblical revelation to the world. Christian schools or Sunday schools that follow the outline of this book can present a mini Bible history in the space of about one year by doing one drama each week.

The dramas are written to help children learn and understand the events of the Bible but they should not stand alone. It is important to note that the presentation of a drama is never intended to replace the proclamation of the Word—it is used to enhance the teaching. While the dramas contain the message of Christ's love for us, children often need help applying that message to their lives. These dramas work best as thought-starters for a children's talk in a chapel, a Bible study, or a group presentation followed by a class session discussing the application of the story.

The dramas were originally written for specific age levels (as noted in the scripts). Feel free to adapt them for whatever age level you are working with. For example, where the script says the children pantomime and all lines are spoken by a narrator, you might want to assign some lines to children. Or, where lines are divided, you might want to give all lines to several narrators and have the children pantomime. The idea is to use the script however it works with your group to help the children learn and understand the events from the Bible, while making the learning *fun*. One way to introduce each sketch is to write the title on a poster board and to diplay it on a tripod where the audience can see it but where it won't be in the way of the action.

Throughout the book, theatrical terminology, such as centerstage, down left, stage right, etc. was used for consistency. If you are unfamiliar with these terms, have no fear—simply use the stage layout on the opposite page to help you. (Note: UR is upstage right or, simply, up right. URC is up right center, and so on.) And remember that these dramas can be performed in any setting: a classroom, the chancel, a multi-purpose room, etc. Adapt the stage directions to work in your own space.

It is my prayer that these dramas help you bring Bible events—some well known, others not—to life for your students.

Grace and peace,

Larry M. Vogel

A Super Scientific World

▚▚▚▚▚▚▚▚▚▚▚▚

Text: Genesis 1:1–31

Level: Grades 4–6

Participants: Narrator, Joe, Merly, Barry

Props: Assorted tools, ladder, stuff of all kinds

Sound: Microphone for Narrator

Notes: The basic theme is the difference between God's creation and ours, God's majestic greatness and our bumbling. Staging can be kept somewhat simple, though lab coats for the three scientists would be great and the more tools and the more stuff, the better. A stepladder is needed and can be brought out when tools are gathered. The three scientists can either memorize their lines or their parts can be mimed and three hidden readers can read the parts. The characters are 3 Stooges knockoffs. Joe is supercilious. Merly is the daffy one. Barry is in between, probably with a very matter-of-fact air.

▚▚▚▚▚▚▚▚▚▚▚▚▚▚▚▚▚▚▚▚▚▚▚▚▚▚

NARRATOR

Once upon a time there were three scientists: Joe, Barry, and Merly. They were wise beyond measure—though one was wiser than the others, as you'll see. Oh, what creativity! What audacity!

JOE

(*Holding a light bulb above his head*) I have a sagacious sapiential envisagement.

MERLY

Goody, goody, goody! … Huh?

BARRY

He has an idea.

MERLY

Goody, goody, goody!

BARRY

Tell us! Tell us, oh brainiac.

JOE

I will. Soon. Very soon. As soon as I find the right words.

BARRY and MERLY both take huge deep breaths. JOE stands grandly and meditatively. BARRY and MERLY gradually begin to stagger and reel as they hold their breath longer and longer.

NARRATOR

With bated breath, Barry and Merly awaited the grand announcement. This took a whole day: the first day. *(ACTORS freeze. Lights dim then come back up.)*

JOE

Eureka! I can now say it precisely! Let us make a world worthy of ourselves!

JOE

(Sung to the tune of "Let's Go Fly a Kite") Let's go make a world,
A super, scientific world.
Let's go make a world just fine and dandy.
One where the air is sweet,
A micro-mathematic feat,
Let's go … make a world!

MERLY/BARRY

Let's go make a world,
A super, scientific world.
Let's go make a world just fine and dandy.
One where the air is sweet,
A micro-mathematic feat,
Let's go … make a world!

NARRATOR

And after an evening and a morning, the plan was begun. And that was the second day.

MERLY

Goody, goody, goody! How're we gonna do this world?

BARRY

Tools! Tools! We need tools!

JOE, MERLY, and BARRY rush around collecting a variety of tools from fix-it tools to microscopes or chemistry/scientific things.

NARRATOR

And so the three geniuses gathered all their tools, and after an evening and a morning, they were finished. And that was the third day.

JOE

There! Now we're ready.

MERLY

Goody, goody, goody! Now that we have the tools, what're we gonna work on???

BARRY

Stuff! Stuff! We need stuff! Lots and lots of stuff.

JOE

Exactly as I was about to say: We need stuff.

JOE, MERLY, and BARRY rush around collecting stuff *from wood, to cardboard boxes, to cloth, to bags of things—anything will do.*

NARRATOR

And so the three geniuses gathered *stuff*, and after an evening and a morning, their stuff was together. And that was the fourth day.

JOE

Now. Let me consider my plan. … Ummmmmmmmmmmmmm … *(after a long, meditative pause)* I have it!

All three whisper together.

BARRY

Sooooooooooo smart. Sheer genius!

MERLY

(To BARRY) Goody, goody, goody! He's so smart. Uh, okay, what is that again?

JOE

The plan, as I have indicated, is that of recombinant TNA, with S.

MERLY

Goody, goody, goody!

BARRY

What-what-what-what?

JOE

Recombinant TNA, with S: Tools Now Applied to Stuff! Use the tools on the stuff!

NARRATOR

And so the three geniuses completed their plan, but by then it was another evening and morning. And that was the fifth day.

MERLY climbs the ladder with a tool. JOE picks up a board. BARRY stands by the ladder with a tool.

NARRATOR

(Walking on stage and talking to crowd) Joe, Merly, and Barry began to assemble their super, scientific world. But it was harder than it looked. *(In slapstick fashion, JOE turns with the board, knocks BARRY down and into the ladder, and MERLY falls off the ladder onto JOE. All freeze in place.)* Joe hit Barry with a board, and Barry bumped into a ladder, and Merly fell off the ladder and knocked Joe silly. And that was the sixth day—and there wasn't anything good to show for all their plans. *(Opening Bible)* In the beginning God created the heavens and the earth. ... *(looking up to face the audience)* and light and darkness, and land and water, and plants and moon and stars and planets, and birds and animals, and man and woman—and you and me. He created the world in six days and He did it without tools, without fumbling or bumbling, and without any *stuff* whatsoever. God spoke, and it was so—just so—and it was all very good.

The Fall into Sin

Text: Genesis 3:1–24

Level: Grades 1–5

Participants: Adam, Eve, one or more Narrators, Snake Voice, a group of children to make the snake

Props: Potted tree, large blanket or sheet to cover the snake, symbolic drawings of a variety of types of fruit that grow on trees.

Notes: Adam and Eve may speak their lines or the Narrator can read the lines while the actors mime actions. Words spoken by God can be read by a separate Reader or by the Narrator.

Setting the Stage: *A tree is centerstage. ADAM and EVE stand by the tree. Children can be other trees, with pictures of different kinds of fruit taped to their shirts and in their hands. A group of children makes up the snake, lined up single file with the person in back holding the waist of the person immediately in front of him or her. A large blanket can be pinned to the snake-train to cover the children. The snake is off to one side as the action begins.*

NARRATOR

In the beginning God created the heavens and the earth *(Genesis 1:1)*. God saw all that He had made, and it was very good *(Genesis 1:31)*. Now the LORD God had planted a garden in the east, in Eden; and there He put the man He had formed. And the LORD God made all kinds of trees grow—trees that were pleasing to the eye and good for food. In the middle of the garden were the tree of life and the tree of the knowledge of good and evil *(Genesis 2:8–9)*. The LORD God took the man and put him in the garden of Eden to work it and take care of it. And the LORD God commanded the man, "You are free to eat from any tree in the garden; but you must not eat from the tree of the knowledge of good and evil, for when you eat of it you will surely die" *(Genesis 2:15–17)*.

SNAKE enters and moves toward the tree. He addresses the audience.

SNAKE

Hello, there. I'm SSSSSSSSSSSSSSSSSSSneaky SSSSSSSSSSSSSnake. Heh heh! Really, I'm sssssssssssso sssssssssssssneaky, I'm SSSSSSSSSSSSSneaky SSSSSSSSSSSSSSSatan.

That's Adam and Eve over there. They think everything is wonderful. God made this beautiful world just for them and all their children. They *think* everything is fine, but they haven't met me yet. I don't like God—I hate Him! And I hate this wonderful world He made!

ADAM moves to the side, tilling. SNAKE crosses to EVE.

SNAKE

Psssssssssst! How'sssssssss it going? My, what a niccccccccccce tree, and what pretty fruit! Did God tell you not to eat any of the fruit from thisssssssssssss tree?

EVE

God said we can have all the other fruit trees, but not this one, or we'll die.

SNAKE

Sssssssssilly girl! Sssssssssssoooo sssssssssstupid! You won't die. Jussssssssssst tasssssssssssste it!

The other trees begin to shake and quiver to warn EVE.

NARRATOR

So when the woman saw that the fruit of the tree was good for food and pleasing to the eye, and also desirable for gaining wisdom, she took some and ate it.

The other trees droop in disappointment.

EVE

Boy, is this good!

NARRATOR

She also gave some to her husband, who was with her, and he ate it. Then the eyes of both of them were opened, and they realized that they were naked; so they sewed fig leaves together and made coverings for themselves *(Genesis 3:6–7).*

ADAM and EVE

YIKES! *(They run and hide behind the tree.)*

NARRATOR

They heard the sound of the LORD God walking in the garden at the time of the evening breeze, and the man and his wife hid themselves from the presence of the LORD God among the trees of the garden. But the LORD God called to the man, and said to him, "Where are you?"

ADAM and EVE come out looking guilty.

ADAM

I heard the sound of You in the garden, and I was afraid, because I was naked; and I hid myself.

NARRATOR

God said, "Who told you that you were naked? Have you eaten from the tree of which I commanded you not to eat?" The man said,

ADAM

The woman whom You gave to be with me, she gave me fruit from the tree, and I ate.

NARRATOR

Then the LORD God said to the woman, "What is this that you have done?" And the woman replied,

EVE

The serpent tricked me, and I ate.

NARRATOR

The LORD God said to the serpent, "Because you have done this, cursed are you among all animals and among all wild creatures; upon your belly you shall go, and dust you shall eat all the days of your life. I will put enmity between you and the woman, and between your offspring and hers; He will strike your head, and you will strike His heel."

SNAKE slithers off.

CLASS

That, by the way, is why even today,
Whether we're Adam and Eve or Amy and Steve,
We listen to sliding, slithering lies,
And Satan's deceptions that mess up our lives,
And forget all the lessons of salvation and love
That God, in His Word, sends us down from above.
But we do hope you noticed the end of the story,
When God gave a wee little glimpse at the glory
To come, when His Son was to enter our space
And smash Satan's head, and save our whole race.

The Flood

Text: Genesis 6:1–9:29

Level: Preschool–Kindergarten

Participants: Reader(s), Noah, Family, Animal Pairs (as many as there are kids)

Props: Some kind of ark (a church pew will work, as will a bench or a large box, such as a refrigerator box); a couple of carpentry tools (hammer, saw); a couple of boards; one or more watering cans; animals can be indicated by drawing or gluing cut-out animal faces on brown paper lunch sacks (then each child could be a pair of animals, holding the pair on his or her hands); one set of white bags drawn to be birds

Sound: Microphones for Narrator and Voice, and lapel microphone for Noah

Notes: Sing the song "Arky, Arky" (author unknown; traditional) interspersed through the reading. Piano accompaniment can be found in *Psalty's Super Songbook* (Waco, Texas: Maranatha Music, 1985) page 19 or in *My Bible Stories: The Hop-Aboard Handbook and Sing-Along Cassette* by Carol Greene (St. Louis, Missouri: Concordia Publishing House, 1993) page 11. If Noah and his family are too young to speak their lines, have another reader do their lines from offstage.

Setting the Stage: *NOAH, centerstage, puts a hand to his ear, listening. At the mention of the flood, NOAH puts his hand over his mouth in surprise.*

Song—Part 1: *(Sung by the entire group)*
The Lord said to Noah, there's gonna be a floody, floody,
Lord said to Noah, there's gonna be a floody, floody,
Get those animals out of the muddy, muddy, children of the Lord.
Refrain: So rise and shine, and give God the glory, glory,
Rise and shine, and give God the glory, glory,
Rise and shine, and give God the glory, glory, children of the Lord.

READER

The LORD saw how great man's wickedness on the earth had become, and that every inclination of the thoughts of his heart was only evil all the time. The LORD was grieved that He had made man on the earth, and His heart was filled with pain. So the LORD said, "I will wipe mankind, whom I have created, from the face of the earth—men and animals, and creatures that move along the ground, and birds of the air—for I am grieved that I have made them." But Noah found favor in the eyes of the LORD *(Genesis 6:5–8).*

VOICE

Noah! I'm planning something. I'm sending a flood. All the people all around you and all the rest of the people all over the world are very, very disappointing to me. They are mean to each other. They think bad things, they talk about bad things, and they *do* bad things. They hate one another. They say the meanest things to each other. And they hurt each other—they even kill each other! All of them! All over! But you and your family are different.

NOAH

Me, different?

FAMILY

Us, different?

VOICE

Yes, you are righteous.

NOAH/FAMILY

What's righteous?

VOICE

I know what you're thinking: You get angry and you say mean things and you hurt each other sometimes too. *(NOAH and his FAMILY nod their heads guiltily.)* I know all about that—but you haven't stopped listening to Me. So you haven't forgotten what is right and wrong. You believe—I forgive. And that makes you righteous in My eyes. I want you and your family to be safe from all the bad things and all those dangerous people. I'm going to wash this whole earth clean and start over with you and the animals you save.

NOAH/FAMILY

Animals? What animals?

VOICE

Just wait, I'll explain in a minute.

Song—Part 2: *(Sung by the entire group)*
The Lord, told Noah, to build him an arky, arky,
Lord, told Noah, to build him an arky, arky,
Build it out of hickory barky, barky, children of the Lord.
Refrain: So rise and shine, and give God the glory, glory,
Rise and shine, and give God the glory, glory,
Rise and shine, and give God the glory, glory, children of the Lord.

READER

So God said to Noah, "I am going to put an end to all people, for the earth is filled with violence because of them. I am surely going to destroy both them and the earth. So make yourself an ark of cypress wood; make rooms in it and coat it with pitch inside and out" *(Genesis 6:13–14)*.

VOICE

Noah! I'm sending a flood, soon. A flood is lots and lots of water. More than a pond. More than a stream. More than a river. More than a lake. More than an ocean. Can you swim?

NOAH

Me, swim?

FAMILY

Us, swim?

VOICE

I guess not. So, that's why you need to build an ark—a great big boat, bigger than your house. Bigger than 20 houses! Make it big enough for you and your family and lots and lots of animals.

NOAH/FAMILY

Animals? What animals?

VOICE

Just wait, I'll explain in a minute.

NOAH and his FAMILY hammer and saw and bang on the ark.

Song—Part 3: *(Sung by entire group)*
The animals, the animals, they came in by twosies, twosies,
Animals, the animals, they came in by twosies, twosies,
Elephants and kangaroosies, roosies, children of the Lord.
Refrain: So rise and shine, and give God the glory, glory,
Rise and shine, and give God the glory, glory,
Rise and shine, and give God the glory, glory, children of the Lord.

READER

"You are to bring into the ark two of all living creatures, male and female, to keep them alive with you" *(Genesis 6:19)*.

Kids march to the ark, making animal sounds or gestures (e.g., hopping, mooing, barking).

VOICE

(Counting as the last animals enter.) … Five hundred thousand and one, five hundred thousand and two, five hundred thousand and three, five hundred thousand and four. There!

NOAH/FAMILY

Look at all these animals!

VOICE

Right. These are the animals I told you about. I wanted them all to be safe—and you too—from those mean people out there.

NOAH

It's starting to rain!

VOICE

Okay. Now, in you go! *(NOAH and FAMILY enter the ark.)*

Kids may stand above the ark sprinkling with watering cans (put a wash basin or something similar out of sight to catch the water).

Song—Part 4: *(Sung by entire group)*
It rained and poured for forty daysies, daysies,
Rained and poured for forty daysies, daysies,
Nearly drove those animals crazies, crazies, children of the Lord.
Refrain: So rise and shine, and give God the glory, glory,
Rise and shine, and give God the glory, glory,
Rise and shine, and give God the glory, glory, children of the Lord.

READER

In the six hundredth year of Noah's life, on the seventeenth day of the second month—on that day all the springs of the great deep burst forth, and the floodgates of the heavens were opened. And rain fell on the earth forty days and forty nights *(Genesis 7:11–12).*

VOICE

Boy, is it ever noisy in there!

NOAH

God? Can we come out now? Send the birds to check it out.

Child with the white bird bags comes out and pretends to fly around, then returns to the ark.

Song—Part 5: *(Sung by entire group)*
The sun came out, and dried up the landy, landy.
The sun came out, and dried up the landy, landy.
Everything was fine and dandy, dandy, children of the Lord.

Refrain: So rise and shine, and give God the glory, glory,
Rise and shine, and give God the glory, glory,
Rise and shine, and give God the glory, glory, children of the Lord.

READER

The waters flooded the earth for a hundred and fifty days. But God remembered Noah and all the wild animals and the livestock that were with him in the ark, and He sent a wind over the earth, and the waters receded *(Genesis 7:24–8:1)*.

ANIMALS exit the ark, followed by NOAH and his FAMILY.

READER

And God sent a rainbow to be a promise that He would never send such a big flood again. The animals and Noah's family all had many babies, and soon the world was full of people and animals again.

The Tower of Babel

~~~~~~~~~~~~~~~~

Text: Genesis 11:1–9

Level: Preschool to Kindergarten

Participants: 1–5 Readers, 3 Leaders, 3 children to mime or speak God's part, Group

Props: Blocks or boxes, some large (Boxes from a moving company work well.)

Notes: This story should be read with pauses for children to enact the different scenes.

Setting the Stage: *A pile of boxes and blocks is off to one side.*

~~~~~~~~~~~~~~~~~~~~~~~~~~~~~~~~~~~~~~

READER

Once, the whole world spoke one language and used all the same words. A group of people moved to a nice flat land and learned how to make bricks and building materials. They were very smart. *And* very dumb.

LEADER 1

(pointing up) Look at the sun!

GROUP

SUN!

LEADER 2

(pointing to a pile of blocks) Look, blocks!

GROUP

BLOCKS!

LEADER 3

Let's build up to the sun!

GROUP

BUILD!

The children pick up the blocks and boxes and build a tower as high as they can reach.

READER

They were so dumb they thought that if they made their tower tall enough, they would be able to get into heaven. They were so *smart* that they could build a tall, tall tower. Who knows how tall it might have been, *but …*

Three children with arms across one another's shoulders ENTER.

READER

Well, God saw their tower, and He was unhappy. "They are so smart! But they use their brains for bad things," He said. So the LORD confused the people. He made them speak different languages.

LEADER 1

Ko loo uh boo uh.

GROUP

Huh?

LEADER 1

(Louder) Ko loo uh boo uh!

The GROUP shrugs their shoulders.

LEADER 2

Eeky ahky ooh!

GROUP

(Louder still) Huh?!

LEADER 2

(Louder) Eeky ahky ooh!

LEADER 3

Mahli nolly ick!

GROUP

Huh?!

LEADER 3

(Louder) Mahli nolly ick!

The GROUP splits into 3 GROUPS, each following one of the LEADERS and repeating the LEADER's phrase as if it makes sense. The GROUPS EXIT in different directions. One person stays, hiding behind the tower.

READER

So the people stopped building their tower to heaven, because they couldn't understand each other. They moved to all kinds of places and made families that spoke their own language. And wherever they went, all around the world, they found that God was there, because there were plenty of things—plants and animals and everything they would need to eat, build homes, and have families. Even though He scattered them all over, God loved every one of them.

Child pushes the tower over.

READER

The Tower of Babel is long gone, but there are still plenty of proud, foolish people who try to do things their way instead of God's way. We're all that way sometimes. But God will never stop loving us.

The Patriarchs

Text: Genesis 17:1–18:33, 21:1–34

Level: Primary and above

Participants: 2 Narrators, Abraham, Sarah, Isaac, Jacob, Esau, 2 Groups

Props: Doll, robes for characters (optional)

Sound: Microphone for Narrator(s)

NARRATOR 1

Once there was a man named Abraham. *(Light up on ABRAHAM.)* He believed in God. *(ABRAHAM kneels.)* Just about everybody else in those days believed in god*s*—they thought there were bunches of gods, but most people had one favorite god or goddess.

Kids in two groups sing competitively to the tune of "My Dog's Better than Your Dog," from the old Ken-L-Ration commercials.

GROUP 1

Our god's better than your god, our god's better than yours. Our god's better 'cause he makes river water, our god's better than yours.

GROUP 2

Our god's better than your god, our god's better than yours. Our god's better 'cause she makes people happy, our god's better than yours.

GROUP 1

Our god's better than your god, our god's better than yours. Our god's better 'cause he makes the sun shine, our god's better than yours.

GROUP 2

Our god's better than your god, our god's better than yours. Our god's better 'cause she makes farms to grow, our god's better than yours.

NARRATOR 2

But Abraham knew there was only one real God, who called Himself the Lord. This God had appeared to Abraham in a mysterious way. He told him to take his wife, Sarah

(SARAH ENTERS and stands by ABRAHAM), and all his servants, and to go to a new land. The Lord told Abraham that he and Sarah would have a son and that through their son all the world would get a great blessing. The Lord also promised that Abraham and his family would have plenty of land and animals for food.

NARRATOR 1

There was just one problem with all of that. Abraham and Sarah were both old—really old! Abraham was 75, and Sarah was 65. They were older than lots of grandmas and grandpas, but they had never had a baby. It seemed impossible for them to have a baby now, but they believed God's promise. They followed God's Word and traveled miles and miles, for days and days, to the new land. *(ABRAHAM and SARAH walk to a new location.)*

NARRATOR 2

But there was no baby. *(ABRAHAM and SARAH shrug their shoulders.)* Abraham and Sarah waited and waited for about 25 more years. Now they were *really* old—he was almost 100, and she was 90. Still no baby! They thought God was playing jokes on them.

NARRATOR 1

But God came one more time. This time He came in person—well, actually, *three* persons. *(THREE PERSONS ENTER.)* Three men came to visit Abraham and Sarah. They looked just like ordinary men, but they could read Abraham's and Sarah's minds! And they promised one more time: "You'll have a son by this time next year."

NARRATOR 2

And they were right! God kept His promise—the real God was real and Abraham's faith in Him was rewarded. *(SARAH picks up doll and the family EXITS.)* After all those years, they had their son.

NARRATOR 1

Then God did something even more amazing! *(ABRAHAM and ISAAC ENTER.)* One day, He told Abraham to go sacrifice his son, Isaac. God told Abraham's to build an altar and to put Isaac on it to be burned!

NARRATOR 2

Abraham was shocked! He would never have done something like that, but he had faith that God would find a way to make even this work out for the best. So Abraham built an altar. *(ABRAHAM puts a bench into place as an altar.)* When Isaac asked what they were doing, Abraham told him God would provide a lamb. Then Abraham put Isaac on the altar. *(ISAAC is put on the altar, ABRAHAM covers his eyes and lifts the knife.)* He was ready to sacrifice Isaac when God spoke:

NARRATOR 1

"Abraham! I am glad that you had enough faith to do this. Look, there's a ram for your sacrifice." *(ABRAHAM picks up ram, takes ISAAC off the altar and puts ram on the altar.)* So Abraham sacrificed the ram that God gave him and Isaac's life was spared.

NARRATOR 2

Isaac eventually had two sons, Esau and Jacob. *(TWO BOYS ENTER.)* And, when Jacob grew up, he had 12 sons and many daughters. *(All the kids ENTER.)* His sons and daughters had many, many children of their own.

NARRATOR 1

So Abraham was a grandpa and Sarah a grandma—and they had more grandkids than they could count! Hundreds and hundreds of grandkids! And all because Abraham and Sarah believed God's amazing promises and listened to God's Word!

(Optional concluding song: "Father Abraham")

Joseph

Text: Genesis 37:1–50:26

Level: Kindergarten–Grade 2

Participants: Joseph, Brothers, Pharaoh, Kids' Chorus, Narrator(s)

Props: A multicolored jacket or shirt or robe; rope; crown for Pharaoh; grocery bags. Signs may be used to help with the story, such as an arrow sign saying "Egypt," a sign that says "Jail," and one that says "Pharaoh's Palace."

Sound: Microphone for Narrator(s)

Setting the Stage: *KIDS' CHORUS and NARRATOR are to one side. JACOB and all his sons except JOSEPH are centerstage.*

NARRATOR

A man named Jacob had 12 sons—count'em: TWELVE!

Kids speak their lines rhythmically.

KIDS' CHORUS

One, two, one-two-three
That's him, and him, and me.
Four, five, four-five-six
There's more?!? Oh, fiddlesticks!
Seven, eight, seven-eight-nine
Make more food for dinnertime
Glory, glory be!
Let's praise the Lord.

Ten and eleven and twelve
Our God is really swell.
Although we fuss and fight
We're His both day and night.
He just loves us so
No matter where you go
He's taking care of you
So praise the Lord!

NARRATOR

Jacob had one, big, happy family. Welllll … maybe *not* very happy. One of his sons was named Joseph. *(JOSEPH ENTERS.)* Jacob thought Joseph was *just wonderful,* and so he gave him the nicest clothes in the family, including a really fancy jacket. *(JOSEPH looks proud.)* Joseph was pretty special. He had funny dreams—and when he dreamed things, they came true! He could also figure out other peoples' dreams.

NARRATOR

One day Joseph had a dream about his family. He dreamed that his whole family would have to obey him and do whatever he said. Joseph's older brothers didn't like that at all! *(KIDS in the pews stand up and glare at JOSEPH.)*

NARRATOR

Later, Joseph's father, Jacob, sent Joseph to check on his older brothers who were all shepherds. *(BROTHERS ENTER; JOSEPH walks toward them.)* They were still mad at Joseph, and when they saw him coming, they decided to get him back. Some wanted to kill him, but the oldest brother knew that was wrong. *(BROTHERS grab JOSEPH and rough him up; but one stands back, shaking his head. Then the other BROTHERS bind JOSEPH.)* They threw Joseph in a hole. Then, before the oldest brother could help him, the other brothers sold Joseph as a slave. *(JOSEPH walks away with one brother, others EXIT to other side. JOSEPH hangs his head as he EXITS.)*

NARRATOR

Joseph was taken away to Egypt, another country far away. *(JOSEPH ENTERS, crosses center and sits down, looking very sad.)* There he was a slave. For a while he was even put in prison. It looked like he might be put to death! Nobody knew about him and nobody cared about him.

NARRATOR

Well, almost nobody. God didn't forget Joseph. Instead, He helped Joseph to figure out some more dreams. When that happened, the king of Egypt found out about Joseph's amazing ability. The king had a dream, and he wanted to know what it meant. *(KING ENTERS, shakes JOSEPH'S hand, and helps him up from his seat.)*

NARRATOR

Joseph figured out the king's dream. He told the king that for seven years Egyptian farmers would grow more food than they ever had before. Then, for seven more years there would be almost no food. If Egypt ate up all the food from the first seven years, then they would starve later. So the king released Joseph from prison and made Joseph his most important helper. *(KING puts his arm around JOSEPH.)*

NARRATOR

Joseph made sure that plenty of food was stored during the seven good years. Then, when the bad years came, Egypt still had food—they even had enough to be able to sell food to people from other countries. Lots of people came to buy food from Joseph. *(TWO KIDS ENTER with grocery bags to buy food.)*

NARRATOR

Guess who finally came to buy food from Joseph: his brothers! They didn't recognize Joseph, but he knew them. *(BROTHERS come for food, which JOSEPH gives.)* Joseph was very powerful and he could have killed them, but he didn't. Instead, Joseph gave them food. Eventually, Joseph told them who he was, and they brought their father to live with him.

NARRATOR

Joseph didn't hurt them because he had learned a lesson. Though his brothers were mean to him, God was good. When they were trying to hurt him, God was making a way for him to be good to lots of people. Joseph discovered that anyone can be mean, but God can even take meanness and make good things happen. Since God was so good to Joseph, he was happy to forgive his brothers.

The opening kids' chant may be repeated.

Fearless Pharaoh FooFoo

〰〰〰〰〰〰

Text: Exodus 5:1–14:31

Level: Grades 1–4

Participants: Narrator, Pharaoh, Pharaoh's Son, Moses, Frogs, Gnats, Bugs, Cows, Locusts, Israelites.

Props: Glass or pitcher and red food coloring; two pieces of poster board; blue cloth or sheet; a whip.

Notes: Use as many children as possible as frogs, gnats, bugs, cows, locusts, and Israelites. Have some children throw Wiffle balls or ping pong balls as hail. The sea is a blue cloth held by two children. The refrain is sung/chanted to the tune used in the children's rhyme "Little Bunny Foo Foo." The words can be printed on poster board and held up for the audience to join in.

Setting the Stage: *PHARAOH is seated on a throne centerstage. He holds a whip. One or two ISRAELITE SLAVES are working fearfully in front of PHARAOH. PHARAOH has his SON by his side. The SON sneers and makes faces throughout the scene. PHARAOH has a clear pitcher or glass of water on a table by his hand. MOSES turns the water red (using food coloring) for the first plague. Other plagues are acted out by individual children hopping like frogs, biting and buzzing, etc. Two or more children stand off to the side, holding a blue cloth or sheet to represent the sea.*

〰〰〰〰〰〰〰〰〰〰〰〰

PHARAOH

I'm the Pharaoh of all Egypt—that's king to you, stupids! And I ain't afraid of anybody!

NARRATOR

Sounds brave and bold, but it might not be too smart! Even though he's king of all Egypt, there's probably Somebody he should respect and even fear enough to obey.

ALL

(Chanted) Fearless Pharaoh FooFoo, rulin' rich old Egypt,
Picking on the Israelites and working them to death.

NARRATOR

When along came the prophet Moses, and he said,

ALL

Fearless Pharaoh FooFoo, I don't like your attitude
Picking on the Israelites and working them to death.

NARRATOR

Let my people go! God is giving you 10 chances, and if you can't learn to behave, He'll drown you in the sea!

ALL

Fearless Pharaoh FooFoo, rulin' rich old Egypt,
Picking on the Israelites and working them to death.

PHARAOH reaches for the glass or pitcher of water, slips food coloring in it—without the audience seeing—so it turns red. He picks up the glass to drink from it, sees that it's turned red, makes a face, and puts the glass back down. This happens as NARRATOR says the next line.

NARRATOR

When along came the prophet Moses—turning the river water red—and he said,

ALL

Fearless Pharaoh FooFoo, I don't like your attitude,
Picking on the Israelites and working them to death.

NARRATOR

God is giving you nine more chances, and if you can't learn to behave, He'll drown you in the sea!

ALL

Fearless Pharaoh FooFoo, rulin' rich old Egypt,
Picking on the Israelites and working them to death.

NARRATOR

When along came the prophet Moses—with flippy, floppy frogs—and he said,

ALL

Fearless Pharaoh FooFoo, I don't like your attitude,
Picking on the Israelites and working them to death.

NARRATOR

God is giving you eight more chances, and if you can't learn to behave, He'll drown you in the sea!

ALL

Fearless Pharaoh FooFoo, rulin' rich old Egypt,
Picking on the Israelites and working them to death.

NARRATOR

When along came the prophet Moses—with dingy, drastic darkness—and he said,

ALL

Fearless Pharaoh FooFoo, I don't like your attitude,
Picking on the Israelites and working them to death.

NARRATOR

God is giving you one more chance, and if you can't learn to behave, He'll drown you in the sea!

PHARAOH

(Shouting) Get out of here! I don't care about you or your people, and I don't ever want to see you again!

ALL

Fearless Pharaoh FooFoo, rulin' rich old Egypt,
Picking on the Israelites and working them to death.

NARRATOR

When along came the angel of God and he said, "It's all over now, Pharaoh. Kiss your future good-bye."

PHARAOH'S SON falls over, dead.

NARRATOR

And out went all the Israelites, and walked right through the sea.

ISRAELITES follow MOSES as he leads them out. Children holding the sea put it down to let MOSES and the others through.

PHARAOH

Hey! They went right through the Red Sea! Well, I can do it too!

NARRATOR

And along came Fearless Pharaoh FooFoo, ready to pick on those Israelites and work them all to death. But God drowned him in the sea.

Children holding the sea put it over PHARAOH.

ALL

Fearless God Almighty, rulin' rich old Egypt,
Guiding all the Israelites and saving them from death!

Wilderness Wandering

~~~~~~~~~~~~~~~~~~

Texts: Exodus 15:22–16:36; 20:1–13

Level: Grades 5–6

Participants: Moses, Israelites, Voice, Narrator

Props: Stick for Moses; rock; branch from a tree; bits of paper for manna

Sound: Microphone for Voice, lapel microphone for Moses

Setting the Stage: *ISRAELITES ENTER following MOSES, wandering slowly and dejectedly. ISRAELITES sing to the tune of "I Wonder as I Wander" Joyful Sounds, (St. Louis, Missouri: Concordia Publishing House, 1977) hymn 19. Use a fan to blow the bits of paper (manna) in or drop them from a bucket above the stage area.*

~~~~~~~~~~~~~~~~~~

ISRAELITES

(Singing) I wonder as I wander all over this sand,
Why God ever took us from old Egypt land.
We're tired and we're thirsty, we barely can stand,
I wonder as I wander—I don't understand.

First God works a wonderful sign of His power.
Then next thing you know your whole life becomes sour.
How could the same God who makes sunrise and flowers,
Forget His whole people, the very next hour?

VOICE

Moses!

MOSES

What?

VOICE

Why are these people complaining?

MOSES

They're all thirsty—there's nothing to drink except some bitter water that tastes terrible.

VOICE

See that piece of wood over there?

MOSES

Yeah, I see it.

VOICE

Toss it in the bitter water.

MOSES

(After throwing it in the water) Hey! The water tastes good now! *(ISRAELITES come to drink. Then they wander around in procession.)*

ISRAELITES

(Singing) We're starving from hunger, there's nothing to eat,
Except a few scraps from our Egyptian feast.
We'll eat almost anything: vegetables, meat …
Although so much better would be something sweet.

VOICE

Moses!

MOSES

What?

VOICE

Now why are these people complaining?

MOSES

They're all hungry—there's nothing to eat.

VOICE

I'm going to make it rain—

MOSES

Rain? Who wants rain?

VOICE

Would you let me finish? I'm going to make it rain some white stuff all over the ground. Tell the people to pick it up, roll it together, and bake it. It will be bread.

MOSES

Great! But is that all they'll get to eat?

VOICE

No ... I'll also send flocks of birds. Tell the people to catch them and cook them—they'll taste better than chicken.

MOSES

Wonderful! *(Pause)* Hey, God?

VOICE

Yeah?

MOSES

What's chicken?

Bits of paper "rain" on the floor. ISRAELITES pick up the bits of paper and mime eating. They continue wandering.

ISRAELITES

(Singing) Our canteens are empty, our water jugs low,
No precipitation, no rain and no snow.
With no milk to drink just how will the kids grow?
Oh, show us a place where wet rivers still flow.

VOICE

Moses!

MOSES

What?

VOICE

What's the matter this time?

MOSES

They're thirsty again.

VOICE

These people! *(Pause)* Okay. Take your staff and walk over to that big rock. Tell the rock to give you some water.

MOSES

Water from a rock? Rocks don't rain.

VOICE

Just do it.

MOSES

Hmmm. I'm going to look like an idiot talking to a rock. But when I hit the Red Sea, it opened up into a road for us to escape Pharaoh. I guess I'll give this a try. *(MOSES hits the rock.)* Wow, look at that—water!

ISRAELITES rush forward and mime drinking. Then they resume their wandering.

ISRAELITES

(Singing) Moses says: "God wants you all to have faith."
All I see is how we just sit and we wait.
If God is so great how come He's always late?
And why is the food all the same on my plate?

VOICE

Moses!

MOSES

What?

VOICE

Don't they *ever* quit complaining?

MOSES

No, never! But You already knew that! You're God—why don't You fix everything? You're really making me mad. I'm sick of this job. We're all ready to give up!

VOICE

Moses, Moses. I'm disappointed in the whole bunch of you. I'm going to have to teach you a lesson. This is for you and the people—but it's also for all your children and grandchildren—all your descendants. They have to learn that even though I do things on My schedule and not yours, that I make things work out right in the end. So I'm not going to let you into the Promised Land—none of you. You can take a peek at it, but you won't get to live there. Your descendants will make it there, but you won't. Maybe they'll be a little better at trust and patience (and not complaining) than your generation is.

NARRATOR

Israel forgot about trusting God, or counting their blessings, because they were too busy whining and complaining and counting all their problems. We're the same way sometimes. And when we are that way, just like Israel, we miss out on all the good things right in front of us. Just as God gave Israel manna every day, He blesses you and me, every single day.

Judges—Again

Text: Judges 4–7

Level: Primary

Participants: Deborah, Barak, Sisera, Jael, Gideon, Narrator, 3 Reading Groups, Enemies

Props: Costumes (optional); toy weapons of any sort; a jar and some type of horn

Sound: Microphone for Narrator(s)

Setting the Stage: *The THREE READING GROUPS ENTER from left. DEBORAH, GIDEON, BARAK, and JAEL should each accompany one of the groups, but **not** read with the group while they are acting: GIDEON with GROUP 1, DEBORAH and JAEL with GROUP 2, BARAK with GROUP 3. SISERA is part of ENEMIES. GROUPS 2 and 3 read rhythmically.*

NARRATOR

Joshua led the people of Israel into the land of Canaan. They learned from him to trust God even though they were weak. He helped them defeat not only Jericho with its great walls, but also other enemies.

GROUPS 1, 2, and 3

But the people were forgetful!

NARRATOR

And when they forgot God, they had problems.

ENEMIES ENTER from right, brandishing weapons.

ENEMIES

We're the problem! Grrrrrrrrrrrrrrrrrrrr! *(ENEMIES EXIT.)*

The THREE READING GROUPS all cower in fear.

GROUP 1

Help, God! Everything is terrible.

NARRATOR

God had to teach them again and again how important it is to trust in Him and to obey Him. When they asked for help, He sent a helper. The people called these helpers "judges." One judge was named Deborah.

DEBORAH and BARAK step to center.

DEBORAH

Hi, I'm Deborah!

BARAK

And I'm her helper, Barak.

GROUP 2

Deborah gave good advice,
She didn't like to fight, 'cause she was nice.

NARRATOR

But along came problems.

ENEMIES ENTER, brandishing weapons.

ENEMIES

We're the problem! Grrrrrrrrrrrrrrrrrrr!

GROUP 1

Help, God! Everything is terrible.

NARRATOR

A mean king named Sisera who hated the people of Israel decided to attack them. *(One boy steps to front of ENEMIES.)*

GROUP 2

God gave Deborah a wonderful plan.
She led the mean king to a hilly land.

NARRATOR

In the hills, her friend Barak was hiding with his army and the soldiers of Israel defeated Sisera's army. *(BARAK and DEBORAH chase ENEMIES offstage, leaving only SISERA.)* Mean Sisera almost got away, but a woman named Jael killed him instead. *(JAEL, part of GROUP 2, kills SISERA.)* Now he couldn't hurt the people of Israel any more.

GROUPS 1, 2, and 3

But the people were forgetful—*again!*

NARRATOR

And when they forgot God, they had problems—*again*!

ENEMIES ENTER, brandishing weapons.

ENEMIES

We're the problem! Grrrrrrrrrrrrrrrrrrr!

GROUP 1

Help, God! Everything is terrible—*again*!

NARRATOR

God had to teach them *again* how important it is to trust in Him and to obey Him. The next judge was named Gideon.

GIDEON steps to center.

GIDEON

Hi, I'm Gideon!

GROUP 3

Gideon was a famous judge,
'Cause he had a faith that wouldn't budge.

ENEMIES come toward the THREE GROUPS, brandishing their weapons and growling.

NARRATOR

Another enemy attacked God's people. They were all afraid because the enemy had many swords and soldiers. They camped very near Israel to rest the night before they planned to destroy the people of Israel. *(ENEMIES lie down and pretend to sleep.)* Although there were thousands of men in Israel's army, God told Gideon to send all but 300 of them away, and He gave them horns and jars instead of swords.

GIDEON sends GROUPS 1 and 2 offstage on the side opposite the ENEMIES. GIDEON hands jars to two members of GROUP 3. They scratch their heads and look at GIDEON like he's crazy.

GROUP 3

When Gideon's horns and jars all crashed,
Midian's army was completely smashed.

NARRATOR

The enemy soldiers woke up to horns blowing and jars crashing to pieces *(GROUP 3 makes as much noise as possible)*, and they were so scared they ran around and killed each other! *(ENEMIES awaken, confused, and run around knocking each other down.)*

GROUPS 1 and 2 ENTER again.

GROUP 1

Before long, the people were forgetful—*again*!

NARRATOR

And when they forgot God, they had problems—*again*!
So God had to teach them ...

GROUPS 1, 2, and 3

again and again and again ...

NARRATOR

to trust Him.

GROUPS 1, 2, and 3

Again and again and again ...

NARRATOR

It's a good thing God is so strong, *and* so patient!

Optional songs: Sing "My God Is So Big" or sing "Again" to the tune of "Amen."

GROUP

Again, again,
Again, again, again.

SOLO

Sing it over.

GROUP

Again, again,
Again, again, again.

SOLO

You need someone to help you.

GROUP

Again.

SOLO

Remember God is with you.

GROUP

Again.

He's always there beside you.

Again, again, again.

GROUP

Sing it over.
Again, again,
Again, again, again.

SOLO

Jesus is our Savior.

GROUP

Again.

SOLO

He's always watching over.

GROUP

Again.

SOLO

He's put our friends beside us.

GROUP

Again, again, again.

GROUP

Sing it over.
Again, again,
Again, again, again.

Samson

Text: Judges 13–16

Level: Preschool

Participants: Samson, Delilah, Philistines, Narrator

Props: Long wig for Samson; boxes for building; long box for top of building; brown and white cloths or ropes.

Sound: Microphone for Narrator(s)

Note: *After the characters introduce themselves, their only speaking throughout the remainder of the sketch will be to repeat a key phrase each time their name is read. Whenever "SAMSON" is read and an asterisk appears, SAMSON should say, "I'm very strong." The same principle goes for DELILAH who says, "I'm gorgeous." And for the PHILISTINES, who say, "We're mean. Yes!"*

NARRATOR

You remember the judges, right? They were the special people God sent to help out when the children of Israel had problems. One couple in Israel during the time of the judges couldn't have babies. They were very sad. God sent an angel to tell the woman that God was going to work a miracle so she could have a child. Then the angel told them not to let their son ever eat anything made from grapes or cut his hair. This was to be a secret that would make the child very, very strong. They soon had a baby boy and named him Samson. They were so thankful for him they obeyed God and Samson didn't eat grapes or drink anything made from grapes or cut his hair. Samson grew up and became very strong.

SAMSON

Hi, I'm Samson. I'm very strong!

DELILAH

I'm Delilah. I'm gorgeous!

PHILISTINES

We're the Philistines—we're mean! Yes!

NARRATOR

The Philistines* were very mean to Israel. They sent their soldiers to steal things from the Israelites and to kill the people. Israel needed a big strong leader like Samson* to help protect them.

SAMSON chases the PHILISTINES away, then sits on one side of the stage. PHILISTINES return to center.

NARRATOR

God helped Samson* to defeat the Philistines* in several battles. That made the Philistine leaders start to think. They decided they would send a beautiful woman named Delilah* to Samson* to figure out how he could be so strong. Maybe Samson* would not be as smart as he was strong.

DELILAH walks over to SAMSON and sits down by him.

NARRATOR

Delilah* was very friendly to Samson*, and he forgot all about being a judge and protecting his people and obeying God. All he could think about was how pretty she was and how much he liked her. Then one day Delilah* asked Samson* to tell her what made him so strong. He lied and told her he wouldn't be stronger than the Philistines* if someone tied him with seven strips of leather. When he went to sleep that night, Delilah* tied him with leather, but it didn't work.

DELILAH ties SAMSON; two PHILISTINES sneak up; SAMSON wakes up, breaks the bonds, and chases them away.

NARRATOR

Delilah* again tried to get Samson* to tell her his secret. Samson* lied again and said that if he was tied with new rope, he would have no power over the Philistines*. When he fell asleep, Delilah* tried that. It didn't work either.

DELILAH ties SAMSON again; two more PHILISTINES sneak up; SAMSON wakes up, breaks the bonds, and chases them away.

NARRATOR

Delilah* tried once more and this time Samson* said if someone braided his hair he would be weak. That didn't work any better than the other things had. Finally, Delilah* told Samson* that if he really loved her, he would tell her his secret. So he told her.

DELILAH pouts and SAMSON leans forward to whisper in her ear.

NARRATOR

While he was sleeping that night, Delilah* cut off his hair.

SAMSON sleeps and DELILAH pulls off the wig.

NARRATOR

This time the Philistines* were stronger than Samson*, and they poked out his eyes and made him a prisoner. They had a party, and everyone laughed at him.

SAMSON stands inside the box house with the PHILISTINES, who point fingers at him and make fun of him.

NARRATOR

Samson* was sorry he had paid more attention to Delilah* than to God. He prayed for God to give him back his strength just one more time. God did just that and Samson* pushed on the walls of the house. It fell down on top of him and all the Philistines*. *(This time instead of saying "We're mean. Yes!" the Philistines say, "We're dead. Oh no!")*

SAMSON pushes on the walls and they fall down, everyone plays dead. No one speaks after this when their name is read.

NARRATOR

Even though Samson died, he defeated the mean Philistines, and the people of God learned a lesson that we should love God more than everyone—even more than a boyfriend or a girlfriend—and that what God says is always best.

Ruth

Text: Ruth

Level: Preschool–Kindergarten

Participants: Narrator(s), Ruth, Orpah, Naomi, Naomi's Husband, 2 Sons, Boaz, assorted Field Hands.

Props: Bench, poster board

Sound: Microphone for Narrator(s)

Setting the Stage: *NAOMI and HER HUSBAND are seated at a bench upstage, center. Three posters may be used to help add emphasis, particularly if the children can't manage the appropriate expressions. One is a circle with a smile in the middle, drawn so that when held the other way, it is a frown. The second poster is a large exclamation point and the third poster is a large question mark.*

NARRATOR

Once there was a woman named Ruth. *(RUTH walks downstage, center.)* When she was little, she didn't know about the real God. She grew up in a country that believed in other gods. She didn't know what to think. *(RUTH shrugs her shoulders.)*

NARRATOR

Ruth had a friend named Orpah. *(ORPAH ENTERS and stands by RUTH.)* They met two brothers who had moved to their country from Israel. *(2 SONS come up to stand by RUTH and ORPAH.)* Ruth and Orpah married the brothers and moved into the house where the brothers lived with their mother and father. The mother was named Naomi. *(RUTH, ORPAH, and 2 SONS cross to sit with NAOMI and her HUSBAND.)*

NARRATOR

Then something terrible happened! *(Show frown poster.)* First, Naomi's husband died. Then one son died. After that, the other son died. Ruth and Orpah were so sad! But Naomi was the saddest one of all. *(NAOMI, RUTH, and ORPAH put their arms around one another.)*

NARRATOR

Poor Naomi had no children and no husband! She lived in a foreign country where she was a stranger to almost everyone. She felt very alone. She was old and needed some-one to help her. Who would help her? She decided to go home to her own country where she had some relatives. What would Orpah and Ruth do? *(Show question mark poster.)* Orpah said she would go along, but then she changed her mind and left Naomi. *(ORPAH EXITS. Poster is lowered.)*

NARRATOR

(NAOMI walks a short distance. RUTH stands centerstage, looking pensive. Show question mark poster.) Now what would Ruth do? Naomi was going far away. Naomi was leaving all of Ruth's family and all of Ruth's friends. Imagine how lonely Ruth would be in a new country. But Ruth would still have Naomi, *and* Ruth would also have Naomi's God. Naomi had taught Ruth all about the real God. Naomi helped Ruth to understand how much God loved her and that God would always take care of her. Even though Ruth would leave her family and her other friends, she knew it was more important to have a friend like Naomi who would help her to know God.

NARRATOR

Ruth said she would go with Naomi, and Ruth did not change her mind. *(RUTH runs to be with NAOMI. Show the exclamation point poster.)* She stayed with Naomi. Ruth wanted to stay with Naomi, and she wanted Naomi's God to stay with her.

FIELD HANDS and BOAZ ENTER and stand down left. They pantomime hoeing or raking.

NARRATOR

Ruth and Naomi traveled a long way to the land of Israel. *(RUTH and NAOMI walk down center.)* Ruth helped Naomi all the way to the new land. Ruth took care of Naomi on the way, and then, when they reached Israel, Ruth *still* helped Naomi. She went out to work in the fields to gather grain to make bread. She cooked for Naomi and she helped Naomi in many ways. *(RUTH crosses over to FIELD HANDS.)*

NARRATOR

Naomi was so thankful for Ruth. Ruth worked hard and helped Naomi in so many ways that Naomi prayed that Ruth would find a wonderful husband. And God answered Naomi's prayer. One day, in the field, a man named Boaz saw Ruth. He was impressed with her because she worked so hard and was so nice to Naomi. He fell in love with Ruth. Then he asked Ruth to marry him. *(BOAZ and RUTH cross down center.)*

NARRATOR

Ruth and Boaz were married. Boaz was very happy! Ruth was very happy too! But the happiest person of all at the wedding ... was *Naomi*! She had another family. *(NAOMI smiles.)*

NARRATOR

Naomi helped Ruth to know God. That made Ruth a very good person and a very good friend. And that helped people who were so sad they didn't know what to do *(ALL ACTORS frown; Show frown poster and question mark poster)* become very happy again *(ALL ACTORS show big smiles; Show smile poster and exclamation point poster)*.

From Cool to Fool

Text: 1 Samuel 9:1–31:13

Level: Grades 1–4

Participants: Narrator(s), Samuel, Saul, Soldier, David, Chorus

Props: Bible; crown; robe; sword; play money

Sound: Microphone for Narrator(s)

Setting the Stage: *SAMUEL is centerstage. The CHORUS is off to one side. When SAUL ENTERS, he should stand between CHORUS and SAMUEL. DAVID will cross down from CHORUS. The title of the drama can be printed on a piece of poster board and placed on a tripod off to one side of the stage.*

NARRATOR

Long ago, in Israel, there was a very wise man named Samuel. Samuel had a strong faith in God, and God used him as His servant. Samuel helped people to know about God, to believe in God, and to obey God. He was a very great leader. But he was also very old.

CHORUS

Too old! Not cool! Sam's a fool!

NARRATOR

Samuel was wise because he knew the things God had said to all the people of the past—Abraham and Sarah and Isaac and Joseph and Moses and Deborah and all the rest. *(SAMUEL opens a Bible.)* He remembered those lessons, and he tried to tell the people what was good and what was bad and all about God and His promises.

CHORUS

Bor-ing! Not cool!

NARRATOR

The people didn't listen to Samuel. They had their own ideas. *(CHORUS turn their backs to SAMUEL.)* They wanted excitement! They wanted fun! They wanted a new leader! They wanted a king—with a crown and an army and a palace and a kingdom!

CHORUS

That's cool!

NARRATOR

Samuel warned them. *(SAMUEL shakes his finger at the CHORUS.)* He warned them that a king might not do what is right and they might not like his laws, but they wouldn't listen.

CHORUS

Kings are cool! Kings are cool! Kings are cool!

NARRATOR

So God told Samuel to let them have their king. He helped Samuel meet a man named Saul *(SAUL ENTERS)*. Saul was not old, he was young! He was not short, he was tall! He was handsome too!

CHORUS

Yeah, Saul! Saul is cool!

NARRATOR

So Saul became their king. *(CHORUS crowns SAUL and puts a robe on him.)* And for a while, Saul listened to Samuel and Samuel listened to God, and everything went pretty well. But then Saul started to ignore Samuel and to ignore God. Saul acted like he didn't need Samuel and he didn't need God. *(SAUL pushes SAMUEL away.)* He did whatever he wanted, and when he wanted advice, he asked anybody but Samuel—even witches!—what he should do. Everything was different.

CHORUS

Different! That's cool!

NARRATOR

Saul made a big army, and lots of young men had to join. *(TWO BOYS step forward from CHORUS; one should be DAVID.)* Saul gave his soldiers lots of weapons and uniforms, and all the people had to pay for them. *(CHORUS hands SAUL a sword.)* Saul did many other things, and the people had to pay for them all. *(CHORUS hands SAUL money.)* Saul was doing whatever he wanted—and the people had problems!

CHORUS

Problems!? Not cool!

NARRATOR

God wanted to help. Samuel was still there. Samuel tried to help, but Saul didn't listen and no one else did either. *(SAMUEL tries to approach SAUL but SAUL pushes him away; SAMUEL leaves his Bible behind.)*

CHORUS

Sam's not cool!

NARRATOR

God still wanted to help, so he sent Saul a helper and a friend named David. *(DAVID crosses to SAUL'S side, opposite SAMUEL.)* David was strong in faith and he was a great helper, but Saul didn't like David either. *(SAUL glares.)*

CHORUS

But, hey, David's cool?!

NARRATOR

Saul wouldn't listen to God. *(SAUL tosses the Bible.)* He wouldn't listen to Samuel. *(SAUL turns his back on SAMUEL.)* And he *hated* David. *(SAUL draws his sword on DAVID.)* Things got worse and worse and worse and worse! Saul's big army started to lose its battles. The young men were killed! *(The SOLDIER behind DAVID falls over, dead.)* All the money was gone! The army was dead! But Saul just made the people send more young men to battle and spend more money.

CHORUS

Not cool! Not cool!

NARRATOR

Before long, nobody thought Saul was cool.

CHORUS

Saul's not cool! Saul's a fool!

NARRATOR

So Saul was sad. He knew something was wrong, but he didn't know what. *(SAUL scratches his head.)* He'd forgotten something. ... He'd forgotten God—he forgot forgiveness. And then, before long, he forgot all hope, and he killed himself! *(SAUL falls over, dead.)*

CHORUS

Yeah, Saul's dead! Saul was a fool! Now everything's cool!

NARRATOR

(Turning to the CHORUS) Saul was a fool, but *not* the only fool! Everyone who thinks cool is what counts is *really* a fool. *(CHORUS hangs their heads.)*

CHORUS

All of us everywhere want to be cool,
Be number one! Be the best in school!
But we better remember the very first rule: *(CHORUS points to themselves)*
When *I* forget God, *I'm* really a fool!
And God won't forget me—now that's *really* cool!

50

BIG Little Man

Text: 1 Samuel 17

Level: Kindergarten–Grade 4

Participants: Narrator, Reader(s), Goliath, David, Philistines, Israelites, Saul

Props: Stepladder (6-foot or larger); sword; grocery bag; slingshot; a large army helmet (or box painted to look like a helmet, or two boxes—one to fit over his body like armor and one for his head); a drawing of two long legs to hang on the front of the stepladder so that when Goliath climbs the ladder he provides the torso and head; poster board (optional)

Sound: Microphone for Reader(s) and Narrator, lapel microphones for David and Goliath

Setting the Stage: *READER is at a microphone. NARRATOR is with group of kids, except DAVID, centerstage. PHILISTINES and ISRAELITES form a group together behind the NARRATOR. After GOLIATH climbs up the ladder, the NARRATOR will step to the side and the group will split into two—one group of PHILISTINES and one group of ISRAELITES.*

If the play is done as part of a series:

NARRATOR

Remember King Saul who was soooo cool, until he became a fool? And remember David, who tried to help Saul? Let me tell you about how king Saul first met David. *(DAVID ENTERS.)* You see, after Saul started being foolish, God knew His people needed a new leader—one who would listen to Him, trust in Him, and obey Him. So God sent David to Saul and eventually made David the next king. David knew how to listen and obey—and especially, David knew how to trust God. Listen to how the story goes in the Bible.

Or, if the play is done individually:

NARRATOR

Long ago, in Bible times, there was a country named Israel with a king named Saul—and they had a very BIG problem: The problem's name was GOLIATH! Listen to this. *(Turning toward READER)*

READER

(Reads from the King James Bible) 1 Samuel 17 says: "Now the Philistines gathered together their armies to battle. ... Saul and the men of Israel were gathered together ... and set the battle in array against the Philistines. And the Philistines stood on a mountain on the one side, and Israel stood on a mountain on the other side: and there was a valley between them. And there went out a champion out of the camp of the Philistines named Goliath, of Gath, whose height was six cubits and a span" *(1 Samuel 17:1–4 KJV).*

KID

(To NARRATOR) Huh? Hey, you: What's a cubit?

NARRATOR

A cubit is a measuring stick they used long ago. Like a ruler—only longer. I'll bet your dad is almost six *feet* tall. That's about this big *(gesturing to six feet on the ladder)*. But Goliath was bigger—*much* bigger *(reaching for the child who will play GOLIATH and helping him onto the ladder).*

GOLIATH

(Stopping on the step that puts his head at about six feet.) About this big?

NARRATOR

No, bigger. *(GOLIATH goes up a step.)*

GOLIATH

This big?

NARRATOR

No, *bigger.* *(GOLIATH goes up another step.)*

GOLIATH

This big?

NARRATOR

No, *bigger.* *(GOLIATH goes up another step—this continues until GOLIATH is either as high as he can go safely, or until his head is at about 10 feet.)*

PHILISTINES and ISRAELITES

That big!?!

GOLIATH

This big! ... And bold! ... And *bad*! You wanna fight me?

PHILISTINES

(Running behind GOLIATH and the ladder) We're on *his* side!

ISRAELITES

(Running in the other direction) We're scared—help!

READER

"[Goliath] had a helmet of brass upon his head, and he was armed with a coat of mail ..." *(Children interrupt the READER who pauses only briefly each time.)*

PHILISTINES

What?

READER

"... the weight of the coat was five thousand shekels of brass. ..."

ISRAELITES

Huh?

READER

"He had greaves of brass upon his legs and a javelin of bronze slung between his shoulders. ..."

PHILISTINES

He had what?

READER

"The staff of his spear was like a weaver's beam, and his spear's head weighed six hundred shekels of iron. ..."

ISRAELITES

(Loudly, befuddled.) What are you talking about?

NARRATOR

Alright! Now listen: Goliath was a huge guy, his armor weighed a ton, and his spear was as big as a telephone pole! Got it?

ISRAELITES and PHILISTINES nod their heads vigorously and fearfully.

READER

Plus, Goliath was as mean as he was big, and he called the Israelites a bunch of wimps, 'cause they were all scared to death.

GOLIATH

I'm Goliath. I'm big! ... And bold! ... And *bad!* You wanna fight me?

PHILISTINES

(Peeking from behind GOLIATH) We're on *his* side!

NARRATOR

So when Saul and the people of Israel heard Goliath roaring and when they saw how big he was, they were scared to death!

ISRAELITES

(Cowering) We're scared—help!

NARRATOR

Everyone in Israel was scared until one day, a boy came from the town of Bethlehem, bringing food for his brothers, who were soldiers in Saul's army.

DAVID ENTERS with a grocery bag. He has a slingshot in his back pocket. He joins the ISRAELITES.

READER

When David came into the Israelite camp, Goliath came up out of the ranks of the Philistines and spoke the same words as before.

GOLIATH

I'm Goliath. I'm big! ... And bold! ... And *bad*! You wanna fight me?

PHILISTINES

(Peeking from behind GOLIATH) We're on *his* side!

ISRAELITES

(Cowering) We're scared—help!

NARRATOR

David saw Goliath, and he saw how afraid all the Israelites were—including his brothers! He was pretty angry.

DAVID

Who does he think he is? Does he think he's stronger than God?

GOLIATH

I'm Goliath. I'm big! ... And bold! ... And *bad*! You wanna fight me?

PHILISTINES

(Peeking from behind GOLIATH) We're on *his* side!

ISRAELITES

(Cowering) We're scared—help!

NARRATOR

David's oldest brother scolded him and tried to send him home. *(One ISRAELITE shakes his finger at DAVID.)* But David wasn't afraid. He knew that God was bigger and better than Goliath. That made David brave. Even though he was only a boy, he asked the soldiers to let him fight Goliath.

READER

And Saul said to David, "Thou art not able to go against this Philistine to fight with him: for thou art but a youth, and he a man of war from his youth." And David said unto Saul, ... [I] slew both the lion and the bear: and this uncircumcised Philistine shall be as one of them, seeing he hath defied the armies of the living God. ... The LORD that delivered me out of the paw of the lion, and out of the paw of the bear, He will deliver me out of the hand of this Philistine" *(1 Samuel 17:33–37 KJV)*.

ISRAELITES

What?!

NARRATOR

That meant David killed a lion and a bear all by himself—which meant he had a lot of faith—which meant he was very brave. Good thing too because Goliath was bigger than a lion and meaner than a grizzly bear!

ISRAELITES

Whoa! Impressive!

GOLIATH

I'm Goliath. I'm big! ... And bold! ... And *bad!* You wanna fight me?

ISRAELITES

Whoa! De-pressive!

PHILISTINES

(Peeking from behind GOLIATH) We're on *his* side!

ISRAELITES

(Cowering) We're scared—help!

DAVID

He's not stronger than God!

READER

So Saul said to David, "Go, and the LORD be with thee!" And Saul armed David with his armor; he put an helmet of brass upon his head, also he armed him with a coat of mail ... *(SAUL puts on the helmet so it covers DAVID'S eyes.)*

NARRATOR

(While these lines are read, DAVID mimes confusion, waving his arms as if he is blind. He stumbles and falls over. Then he removes the helmet and armor.) Poor David couldn't

wear all that big armor—he couldn't even walk with it on. So he took it all off and took out his slingshot and found five smooth, round stones—and he went to face Goliath.

GOLIATH

I'm Goliath. I'm big! ... And bold! ... And *bad*! You wanna fight me?

PHILISTINES

(Peeking from behind GOLIATH) We're on *his* side!

ISRAELITES

(Cowering) We're scared—help!

READER

The Philistine ... drew near unto David. ... When [he] saw David, he disdained him: for he was but a youth. ... The Philistine said unto David, "Am I a dog, that thou comest to me with [stones]?" And [he] cursed David by his gods. [And he said:] "Come to me, and I will give thy flesh unto the fowls of the air, and to the beasts of the field" *(1 Samuel 17:41–44 KJV)*.

NARRATOR

Goliath thought David was a joke! A baby! A wimp!

GOLIATH

I'm Goliath! I'm big! ... And bold! ... And *bad*! You wanna fight me?

PHILISTINES

(Peeking from behind GOLIATH) We're on *his* side!

ISRAELITES

(Cowering) We're scared—help!

NARRATOR

But David went right up to the Philistine and said,

READER

"I come to thee in the name of the LORD of hosts, the God of the armies of Israel, whom thou hast defied" *(1 Samuel 17:45 KJV)*.

PHILISTINES and ISRAELITES

He's crazy!

NARRATOR

Then David took out a stone, slung it, and knocked Goliath right in the head!

GOLIATH

(With his hand on his forehead) I'm Goliath! I'm big, and bold and I have a *bad* headache.

GOLIATH "falls" off the ladder and the ladder is turned over on its side (Orchestrate this stunt carefully so no one gets hurt!).

ISRAELITES

(Running to stand by DAVID) We're on *his* side!

PHILISTINES

We're scared—Help! *(PHILISTINES run away.)*

READER

So David prevailed over the Philistine with a sling and a stone, striking down the Philistine and killing him; there was no sword in David's hand.

NARRATOR

So with a little stone and a great God, David defeated Goliath and the Israelites chased the Philistines away. And David showed how mighty even the smallest person can be when that person trusts in God.

What's Up, Rock?

Texts: 1 Samuel 16:1–23, 18:1–30, 24:1–26:25, 2 Samuel 22:1–51, Psalm 18

Level: Preschool and above

Participants: Narrator(s), Reader, Chorus (Michal and Jonathan are part of the chorus when not playing their parts), Saul, David, Michal, Jonathan

Props: Sword for Saul; Yosemite Sam beard for Saul (optional); guitar; loaf of bread; piano bench or other prop to use for bed; costumes (optional); mock altar (optional); poster board (optional)

Sound: Microphone for Narrator(s) and Reader, lapel microphones for David and Saul

Setting the Stage: *In this retelling of the story, DAVID resembles Bugs Bunny and SAUL parallels Yosemite Sam. Encourage the child who plays DAVID to mimic Bugs Bunny's way of talking, and the same for SAUL with Yosemite Sam. READER and NARRATOR are at microphones. The CHORUS needs to be well-coached to give a cheerleader effect.*

NARRATOR

You remember how David killed Goliath, don't you? Everyone in Israel was happy when he did that. They all cheered and sang and danced for joy. They thought David was wonderful!

CHORUS

(Cheering like cheerleaders) David, David, he's our man!
If Saul can't do it, David can!

NARRATOR

But David was famous for more than fighting. He was also a famous singer, and David prayed a lot too. He turned prayers into songs. One of his song-prayers goes like this:

READER

Psalm 28, verse 1: "To You I call, O LORD my Rock; do not turn a deaf ear to me."

NARRATOR

David often called God his "Rock"—that was one of David's favorite nicknames for God because God was solid and strong, a great big, powerful Rock! David knew it was God, the Rock, who had made his little rock strong enough to kill Goliath. So whenever David was scared or didn't know what to do, he prayed.

DAVID ENTERS, folds his hands, and looks up.

DAVID

Ehhhh, what's up, Rock? I need help!

DAVID picks up guitar, SAUL ENTERS.

NARRATOR

For a while, David sang his songs about God, the Rock, for King Saul.

NARRATOR

David's songs also made him popular with the people.

SAUL glares at DAVID as the chorus praises him.

CHORUS

David, David, he's our man!
If Saul can't do it, David can!

NARRATOR

Even though King Saul liked David's songs, he started to hate David!

While DAVID strums the guitar for the CHORUS, SAUL takes on a boiling pose with fists clenched, arms held rigidly at his sides. He looks angry.

SAUL

(Loudly) Tarnation! David really bugs me.

NARRATOR

After a while, Saul hated David so much he tried to kill him!

Roaring, SAUL rushes toward DAVID with his sword. SAUL chases DAVID back and forth across stage several times. As SAUL chases DAVID, SAUL is crying "Tarnation!"

DAVID runs off.

SAUL

(Pauses from chasing DAVID. He is out of breath.) Tarnation! David really bugs me!

SAUL EXITS. DAVID runs in again, pausing for:

NARRATOR

Poor David, even though the people loved him ...

CHORUS

David, David, he's our man!
If Saul can't do it, David can!

NARRATOR

King Saul hated him!

SAUL ENTERS, sees DAVID.

SAUL

Tarnation! David really bugs me!

DAVID

(Looking up) Ehhh, what's up, Rock? I need help!

SAUL chases DAVID offstage.

NARRATOR

And God—the Rock—did help. God helped king Saul to remember that David was never mean to him. So King Saul told David that if he would fight the Philistines, Saul would let David marry his daughter Michal. David won the battles and soon married Saul's beautiful daughter Michal. He was even more popular.

SAUL, MICHAL, and DAVID ENTER, with MICHAL and DAVID arm in arm.

CHORUS

David, David, he's our man!
If Saul can't do it, David can!

NARRATOR

For a while, Saul was okay. But, before long, Saul became angry again with David.

SAUL glares at DAVID.

SAUL

Tarnation! David really bugs me!

DAVID

Ehhhh, what's up, Rock? I need help!

NARRATOR

Michal loved David, and she helped him to escape from Saul.

SAUL starts for DAVID; MICHAL blocks him, allowing DAVID to escape. SAUL chases. MICHAL EXITS to CHORUS.

NARRATOR

Even though Saul hated him, David didn't hate Saul back. David was brave and fought the Philistines, Saul's enemies. *(JONATHAN and DAVID ENTER with arms over each other's shoulders.)* He was also best friends with Jonathan, Saul's own son. Jonathan and David fought the Philistines together, and the people loved it.

CHORUS

David, David, he's our man!
If Saul can't do it, David can!

SAUL ENTERS.

NARRATOR

That just made Saul hate David even more!

SAUL

Tarnation! David really bugs me!

DAVID

(Looking up) Ehhhh, what's up, Rock? I need help!

NARRATOR

Saul didn't stop chasing David, but God, David's Rock, protected him again. *(SAUL starts for DAVID, but JONATHAN gets in his way, allowing DAVID to escape, followed by SAUL. JONATHAN rejoins CHORUS.)* Saul just became angrier! You'd think David would hate Saul. But he didn't. David could have killed Saul many times. Once, while Saul was sleeping, David was so close he could have killed Saul easily.

SAUL ENTERS, lies down on piano bench or other prop, pretending to sleep. DAVID approaches and picks up SAUL'S sword, looking down at SAUL with the sword in his hand.

NARRATOR

Saul had been so mean to David!

CHORUS

Kill him, David, kill him!

NARRATOR

Saul had tried to kill David again and again.

CHORUS

Kill him, David, kill him!

NARRATOR

Saul had chased David away from his family and friends.

CHORUS

Kill him, David, kill him!

DAVID

(*Looking up*) Ehhh, what's up Rock? Should I kill him?

NARRATOR

(*DAVID lays down the sword and steps back.*) David knew the Rock, his God, would never want him to murder someone. So he didn't kill Saul. And the Rock, who had protected David, now spared Saul's life too.

SAUL

(*SAUL wakes up, looks at DAVID, and then shakes his hand.*) What's up, Rock? Do you love·me too?

NARRATOR

In the end, Saul stopped chasing David. He no longer tried to kill him. And David learned that no matter what, you can always count on the Rock—our God—our Protector, day and night.

Optional closing song, sung to the tune of "Rock around the Clock." Children make a chorus line, with SAUL on one end and DAVID on the other. They all sing:

CHORUS

One o'clock, two o'clock, three o'clock Rock
Four o'clock, five o'clock, six o'clock Rock
Seven o'clock, eight o'clock, nine o'clock Rock
You got a Rock who's with you day and night!

Lots to do, ya gotta run
He's right there when you're havin' fun
He's standin' by your side in the mornin' light
He's gonna still be there when it's dark tonight
You got a Rock who's with you mornin', noon, and night.

One o'clock, two o'clock, three o'clock Rock
Four o'clock, five o'clock, six o'clock Rock
Seven o'clock, eight o'clock, nine o'clock Rock
You got a Rock who's with you day and night!

Out o' bed, gonna start your day
Some gotta work while others play
You can be old or young or in between
It don't matter none—it's all His scene
You got a Rock who's with you mornin', noon, and night.

One o'clock, two o'clock, three o'clock Rock
Four o'clock, five o'clock, six o'clock Rock
Seven o'clock, eight o'clock, nine o'clock Rock
You got a Rock who's with you day and night!

10 P.M., another run to the store
He's right there and forevermore
You got a Rock around you all the night
You got a Rock right there in the broad daylight
You got a Rock who's with you mornin', noon, and night.

One o'clock, two o'clock, three o'clock Rock
Four o'clock, five o'clock, six o'clock Rock
Seven o'clock, eight o'clock, nine o'clock Rock
You got a Rock who's with you
Ev'ry day and night!

Solomon—Wise for a While

Texts: 1 Kings 1:1–11:43

Level: Preschool and above

Participants: Narrator(s), Reader, Solomon, 3 Wives' Groups

Props: Crown for Solomon, perhaps also for the 3 queens; blocks of some type for buildings (Large cardboard boxes covered with brown or white butcher paper work well.)

Sound: Microphones for Narrator(s), Reader, lapel microphone for Solomon

Setting the Stage: *READER and NARRATOR are adults and move freely throughout this skit, helping the children build the temples. SOLOMON is centerstage. The other children are in three groups, off to one side, perhaps seated in three pews or on benches. Each of SOLOMON's WIVES has one group. Boxes are either offstage or hidden out of the view of the audience.*

Part 1—Solomon Prays for Wisdom

NARRATOR

(Moving to stand next to SOLOMON) Meet Solomon. When David was very old, he chose his son, Solomon, to be the next king. So Solomon became king. *(Moving off to the side)* But Solomon was very scared. He didn't know what to do, so he asked for God's help.

SOLOMON

Help!

NARRATOR

Solomon thought he was too young to be king.

SOLOMON

Help!

NARRATOR

Solomon thought there were too many people for him to rule.

SOLOMON

Help!

NARRATOR

Sooooooo … Solomon prayed.

SOLOMON kneels down and folds his hands.

READER

(1 Kings 3:6–14, paraphrased and condensed) Solomon said, "O LORD my God, You have made Your servant king in place of my father David, although I am only a little child; I do not know how to go out or come in. And Your servant is in the midst of the people whom You have chosen, a great people, so many they cannot be counted. Give me an understanding mind to govern Your people, so I am able to discern between good and evil; for who can govern this Your great people?"

NARRATOR

So Solomon got what he wanted, and it was a good thing. *(SOLOMON stands.)* God made Solomon wise and understanding. Solomon's wisdom helped him to lead the people of Israel and be a good king for a long, long time. *(GROUPS cheer.)*

Part 2—Solomon Builds the Temple

NARRATOR

God blessed Solomon in so many ways that he wanted to help all the people to know about God, trust in God, worship God, and obey God. Solomon really wanted to help.

SOLOMON

I want to help!

NARRATOR

So Solomon remembered that his father, King David, wanted to build a temple to help the people remember God. That would be a good thing.

SOLOMON

I want to help!

NARRATOR

So Solomon decided to build a big, beautiful temple to help the people remember God and be forgiven by God.

SOLOMON

I want to help!

NARRATOR

So he did. He built a beautiful temple, and whenever the people went there to sacrifice and pray, God forgave them. What a big help Solomon's temple was!

Children from GROUPS each pick up one box, carrying it to the center to build the temple.

READER

(1 Kings 8:23) When Solomon finished building the temple, he prayed. He said, "O LORD, God of Israel, there is no God like You in heaven above or on earth below—You who keep Your covenant of love with Your servants who walk before You with all their heart. *(1 Kings 8:28–30, paraphrased and condensed)* Hear my prayer, O LORD my God, so Your eyes are open night and day toward this house, where You said, 'My name will be there,' and answer my prayer and the prayers of Your people Israel when they pray in this place; hear us and forgive our sins."

NARRATOR

So Solomon got what he wanted, and it was a good thing. God gave him great wisdom and an understanding mind. Solomon's wisdom helped him to build a beautiful temple for God and his people.

Part 3—Solomon Builds Idol Temples

NARRATOR

God blessed Solomon in even more ways. God wanted to make Solomon a wiser and better king. But, as Solomon grew older, he didn't get wiser. He didn't want God's help—he didn't want any help.

SOLOMON

I don't want any help.

NARRATOR

Solomon forgot about God and His wisdom. He married many women. One *(WIFE ONE ENTERS)* right *(WIFE TWO ENTERS)* after *(WIFE THREE ENTERS)* another. They all believed in different gods and didn't believe in the real God. How could Solomon keep them all happy?

SOLOMON

I don't want any help.

NARRATOR

So Solomon decided he would make his wives happy by building them temples for the different gods they believed in. He didn't ask for God's help.

SOLOMON

I don't want any help!

NARRATOR

So Solomon built beautiful temples for the other gods that his wives believed in—many temples for many gods.

During the following reading, each WIFE in turn takes children from her group and they remove blocks from the temple and arrange them in three small stacks to build three other temples.

READER

(1 Kings 11:3–8, paraphrased and condensed) Solomon soon had seven hundred wives and three hundred girlfriends. And the more he loved them, the less he loved God. As Solomon grew older, his wives turned his heart away from God, and he began to follow and worship other gods. His heart was not true to the LORD his God. Solomon followed Ashtoreth, the goddess of the Zidonians, and Milcom, the god of the Ammonites. So Solomon did what was evil to the LORD and did not follow the LORD completely, as his father, David, had done. Solomon built temples for false gods and made places for his wives to offer incense and sacrifices to their gods.

NARRATOR

So Solomon got what he wanted again—and it wasn't a good thing. God let him build the temples for false gods. Solomon was no longer wise and understanding. Solomon's foolishness now helped to lead many of the people of Israel away from God, and they began to worship the false gods too. Solomon wasn't very wise in the end. But maybe we can be wiser because of him. The good things Solomon did when he was wise could all be undone when he became foolish. The worst thing of all was that Solomon forgot the real God, who forgives sins and helps foolish people become wise again.

Optional closing song (sung to the tune of Roy Orbison's "Crying over You"). Portions in parentheses can be sung by a backup chorus in 1960s rock style.

Solomon, Wise for a While

> I was so wise, for a while, I was a whiz for a while
> But then I closed up my heart and before long had a start
> At being truly ignorant
> It was something to see, the big change in me
> And now I'm clueless (Foolish, too.)
> Senseless (Yes, that's true.)
>
> I once was discreet, so rational and complete.
> (But now he's truthless, foolish, clueless, clueless …)
> I'm clueless—oh so clueless—Clueless as can be.
>
> What could be wrong? Why is this song such a sad hopeless tune?
> I know that somewhere something I used to know is missing.
> Something that's gone so now I'm blue.
> The thing that made me so wise—how could I lose such a prize,
> And become clueless … (Foolish too.)
> Senseless (Yes, that's true.)
>
> I once was discreet, so rational and complete.
> (But now he's truthless, foolish, clueless …)
> I'm clueless—oh so clueless—Clueless as can be.

Rehoboam Rubs 'Em Wrong

Text: 1 Kings 12:1–33

Level: Grades 5–6

Participants: Narrator(s), Solomon, Tax Man/Woman, Rehoboam, Jeroboam, Conscience/Devil (same actor), Israelites

Props: 2 paper crowns and a throne (elevated chair); a tax collector booth (may consist of no more than large sign or poster in a visible spot that reads, "Pay Your Taxes Here," with the Tax Collector located behind it); play money; two pictures, one of a devil and one of an angel for Conscience to use

Sound: Microphone for Narrator(s) and Conscience/Devil; lapel microphones for Tax Man and Jeroboam

Setting the Stage: *NARRATOR(S) stand at their microphone(s). ISRAELITES are centerstage, lined up at the tax booth. JEROBOAM is part of the ISRAELITES at first. REHOBOAM is offstage. SOLOMON is seated on a throne behind the crowd, elevated if possible.*

NARRATOR

You remember Solomon, don't you? The older he grew, the more wives he wanted. The more wives he got, the more temples they wanted. The more temples they wanted, the more money he needed. The more money he needed, the more taxes he charged!

TAX MAN

Step right up and pay your taxes! Our great and wonderful king needs your money!

One by one, the ISRAELITES step forward and hand over money to the TAX MAN, then step to the side, gradually forming a group. To each person TAX MAN says:

TAX MAN

Not enough! Not nearly enough!

ISRAELITES

(Sung to the tune of "Heigh-ho" from Snow White and the Seven Dwarfs.*)*
Oh no! We owe! So off to work we go.

Old Solomon is not much fun, oh no, oh no, oh no.
He taxes each and ev'ry single one
We pay the bills for Solomon, oh no, oh no!

ISRAELITES disperse across the stage and pantomime different types of work.

NARRATOR

So the Israelites worked harder and harder to pay more and more taxes. And they liked Solomon less and less.

SOLOMON falls off the throne. All the ISRAELITES turn and stare with their hands over their mouths. Four ISRAELITES come forward and carry SOLOMON off. They return with REHOBOAM, put him on the throne, and place the crown on his head.

NARRATOR

Finally, Solomon grew old and died. After his death, one of his sons, Rehoboam, became the king. The people were very glad to have a new king. *(ISRAELITES cheer and clap.)* They hoped Rehoboam would make their lives a little easier.

JEROBOAM walks up to REHOBOAM. CONSCIENCE steps behind REHOBOAM on the throne, crouching at first.

JEROBOAM

Hi, King! Your father charged us an awful lot for taxes! Do you think you could lower them a little?

REHOBOAM poses as "The Thinker," meditatively. CONSCIENCE stands first to his right side, holding up the angel picture.

CONSCIENCE/DEVIL

Jeroboam is right. You really should lower the taxes. Give the people a break. Don't be so selfish and greedy! Remember how wise your father *used* to be—how he just tried to obey God and be a good ruler to *help* the people. That's the way you should be.

CONSCIENCE/DEVIL

(Moving to the other side, holds up the devil picture) Stuff and nonsense! Don't listen to that guy, Jeroboam. You have to prove how tough you are! You show them that you're even tougher than your father. Come on! Lay down the law and pile on the taxes!

CONSCIENCE crouches down out of sight again. REHOBOAM breaks his "Thinker" pose and holds up one finger as if he has a great idea.

NARRATOR

So Rehoboam made a decision. Was it the right one? Noooooooooooooo! He decided he would *raise* the taxes and charge the people even more!

TAX MAN

Step right up and pay your taxes! Our great and wonderful king needs your money!

One by one, the ISRAELITES step forward and hand over money to the TAX MAN, then step to the side, gradually forming a group. To each person TAX MAN responds:

TAX MAN

Not enough! Not nearly enough!

ISRAELITES

Oh no! Re-ho Bo-am has now become
(sung) A more expensive King to fund, oh no, we owe, oh no
Under his thumb, it's worse than Solomon
There's nothing left with Re-ho-bum, oh no, oh no!

ISRAELITES disperse across the stage and pantomime different types of work.

NARRATOR

So the Israelites worked harder and harder to pay more and more taxes. And they liked Rehoboam less and less. Soon after Rehoboam raised the taxes, the people began to complain. They didn't like King Rehoboam, and some of them decided that it would be a good idea to have a new king—Jeroboam!

ISRAELITES

Heigh-ho! You know, We all like Jer-o-boam *(combine last two syllables to bome)*
(sung) He's on our side, He'll sympathize, Heigh-ho! Heigh-ho! Heigh-ho!
He'll save our states by lowering the rates
We need a king like Jer-o-boam, Heigh-ho! Heigh-ho!

The ISRAELITES divide into groups, one gathered around JEROBOAM and one gathered around REHOBOAM.

NARRATOR

Rehoboam was really angry—so angry he was ready to fight—ready to start a war with Jeroboam for leading a rebellion.

REHOBOAM strikes the "Thinker" pose again, looking angry.

CONSCIENCE/DEVIL

(Holding up the angel picture) Don't start a war, Rehoboam! Don't do it! Don't forget who raised those taxes! Let them all go to their homes and earn a living in peace. They aren't your enemies. They're your brothers and sisters.

CONSCIENCE/DEVIL

(Holding up the devil picture) Stuff and nonsense! Prove how tough you are! Get your army together and go kill Jeroboam and all the people who are following him!

NARRATOR

This time Rehoboam listened to the right advice. He calmed down and grew a little wiser. He didn't go to war with his countrymen. He didn't attack Jeroboam. And, just maybe, he remembered that God wants kings, and each of us, to do what we can for one another instead of proving how tough and mean we can be.

Elijah's No Good, Horrible, Very Bad Job

Text: 1 Kings 19:1–18

Level: Grades 3 and above

Participants: Narrator, Helper, 8 Kings, Elijah, Angel, Signholder(s)

Props: Plate of food; 2 small posters; 3 large sheets of poster board; markers

Sound: Microphones for Narrator and Helper, lapel microphones for Elijah and Angel

Notes: *Prepare a sign that reads: "He's got a No Good, Horrible, Very Bad JOB!" The sign is held up by one person whenever the phrase is to be repeated. A second sign, reading "7,000," and a third saying, "He's got a real good, wonderful, very great GOD!" will be used at the very end of the sketch. A teacher, pastor, or director can introduce the sketch and tell the audience that whenever a sign is held up, the audience should read it out loud. A practice session with the first sign would help. One small poster reads "Money!" and the other "More Money!" A pun on Elijah is used throughout, pronounced eh-LIE-just.*

Setting the Stage: *NARRATOR stands stage right. The HELPER is stage left, next to ELIJAH (who is frozen). Two KINGS, with their backs pressed together, are centerstage, with one facing the audience and the other (smaller) KING, somewhat concealed behind the first.*

NARRATOR

Sometimes things go from bad to worse. And sometimes, when you think things can't get any worse, you find out that they can get a lot worse.

HELPER

Even in the Bible?

NARRATOR

Yes, that's the way it was for God's people for a long, long time. When Solomon was king, things got bad—the people had to pay really high taxes. They thought it couldn't get any worse. *(KING 1 begins to glare at the audience and holds up the sign saying*

"Money," then passes it behind himself to the hidden KING 2.) But Solomon's son taxed them even more! *(KING 1 looks even meaner and holds up the small sign reading: "More money!")* Then, along came Jeroboam and the kingdom split into two parts with two kings. *(KINGS 1 and 2 rotate 90 degrees so that both are sideways to the audience, then each takes two steps away from the other. They turn to glare at each other.)* Now the country was divided! And the people still had to pay taxes! *(KINGS 1 and 2 hold up the signs saying, "Money" and "More Money.")*

HELPER

That's bad.

NARRATOR

But it gets worse. Then, Jeroboam started to tell the people in his half of the country not to go to the temple Solomon had built in Jerusalem. So they began to worship false gods. *(KINGS glare at each other and then EXIT on opposite sides.)*

HELPER

That was worse than before!

NARRATOR

So bad you'd think it couldn't get any worse ... but it did! Most of the kings who came after Rehoboam in the southern kingdom, called Judah, were bad. And *all the kings* who ruled in the northern kingdom—after Jeroboam—got worse and worse!

HELPER

Oh no!

NARRATOR

Oh yes! First, Nadab ... *(KING 3 ENTERS, looking mean)* who was bad, then Baasha ... *(KING 4 ENTERS while KING 3 EXITS)* who was really bad, then Elah ... *(KING 5 ENTERS while KING 4 EXITS)* who was awful.

HELPER begins to hold his head, feigning a headache.

NARRATOR

Then Zimri ... *(KING 6 ENTERS and pretends to kill KING 5, then KING 6 kills himself)* who killed Elah and then killed himself. And then Omri ... *(KING 7 ENTERS)* who was as bad as all the rest ... and then came Ahab! *(KING 8 ENTERS while the other KINGS EXIT.)*

HELPER

What a headache!

KING 8 EXITS.

NARRATOR

As bad as it was, God didn't give up on His people. Instead, He sent a prophet. A prophet is a person with a message from God. The prophet's name was Elijah.

HELPER

This is Elijah. Strange name, right? How'd you like to be named Elijah ... it means something, but I forget what ... All I know is Eli-just can't take his life anymore!

ALL

He's got a no good, horrible, very bad job!

NARRATOR

Elijah was a prophet—a real one. God told him to be a prophet—it wasn't Elijah's idea! Being a prophet sounds pretty cool, right?

ELIJAH

WRONG!

HELPER

Eli-just can't take it anymore!

ALL

He's got a no good, horrible, very bad job!

ELIJAH

It STINKS!

NARRATOR

Anyone know what a prophet is—a real one? It's somebody who talks for God. Somebody who tries to tell people what God says.

HELPER

It's like being God's *mouth*, right? Well ... everybody just calls Elijah *Bigmouth*! *Eli-just can't take it anymore!*

ALL

He's got a no good, horrible, very bad job!

ELIJAH

I CAN'T STAND IT!

NARRATOR

Elijah had to obey God. He had to try to tell people what's right, you know?

HELPER

So what do they do? They call him names! They tell him to shut up. They're sick of him and what he has to say.

ELIJAH

Queen Jezebel is out to kill me!

NARRATOR

Everybody thinks he's some kind of religious freak.

ELIJAH

I *feel* like a religious freak! Nobody else believes this stuff. It's just me, and everybody hates *me*! I'm gonna eat some worms!

HELPER

Eli-just can't take it anymore!

ALL

He's got a no good, horrible, very bad job!

ELIJAH

I want a transfer!

NARRATOR

All the other prophets hated him. Ahab, the king, hated him.

ELIJAH

And the queen *really* hates me! And it's all God's fault!

HELPER

Eli-just can't take it anymore!

ALL

He's got a no good, horrible, very bad job!

ELIJAH

(*Shouting*) I'm gonna move to Australia! Or maybe the wilderness.

ELIJAH crosses centerstage.

NARRATOR

So, Elijah ran away to the wilderness. He was all alone. He had no friends.

HELPER

His sister hates him—she calls him "Pizzaface." His brother hates him—he beats him up.

ELIJAH

My parents don't even like me. Everybody thinks I'm a religious NUT!

HELPER

Eli-just can't take it anymore!

ALL

He's got a no good, horrible, very bad job!

ELIJAH

(Crying loudly) I WANNA DIE! WAAAAAAAAAAAAAAAHHHHHHHH!

ELIJAH (or offstage voice) sings the following stanza to the tune from Roy Orbison's "Crying over You."

ELIJAH

I was alright, for awhile.
I could smile, for awhile
But now the Queen's on my case
And I'm the one they all hate
And God is nowhere to be found.
Is it a wonder why, I just want to die?
Or why I'm crying, over me? Crying, over me?
When God said, "So long,"
And left me standing all alone.
Alone and crying, crying, crying.
I'm crying, crying, crying over me.

ELIJAH bursts into tears after or during the song ... perhaps throws a tantrum; then falls asleep.

NARRATOR

Things were really bad for Elijah. He felt all alone. But God didn't forget Elijah. He came to comfort Elijah. He sent His angel.

ANGEL ENTERS, crosses to ELIJAH and gives him food.

ANGEL

Eat, Elijah!

ELIJAH scarfs down the food.

ELIJAH

I feel a little better, but I've still got a no good, horrible job!

ANGEL takes him stage left (farther into the wilderness) and sits him down.

ANGEL

Look, Elijah, you probably don't know this, but God has prepared three helpers for you, good ones too! Their names are Jehu, Elisha, and Hazael.

ELIJAH

Oh no! More strange names!

ANGEL

Back off, Elijah. They're good guys, and they're on God's side too.

ELIJAH

Oh well, alright … Gee, thanks. But I've still got a no good job!

ANGEL helps him up and then tells him about the 7,000.

ANGEL

Yeah well, know what else? You're not nearly as alone as you thought. There are over 7,000 other believers trying to do what you said. That's a seven and *three* zeroes!

Signholder holds up the 7,000 sign.

ALL

Seven thousand!

ELIJAH

Seven thousand! Well … maybe … possibly … it could be … I guess I might make it after all!

NARRATOR

Because …

ALL

He's got a real good, wonderful, very good God!

NARRATOR

And more friends than he thought!

An Ahab Headache
and a Jezebelly Ache

Text: 1 Kings 21:1–29

Level: Primary

Participants: Narrator, Helper, Ahab, Jezebel, Naboth, 2 Liars, Group

Props: Two chairs for thrones; crowns; grapes

Sound: Lapel microphones for Ahab and Jezebel; stand microphones for Narrator and Helper.

Setting the Stage: *NARRATOR stands stage right. HELPER is stage left. Two thrones are centerstage. AHAB is on one throne. When JEZEBEL ENTERS, she sits on the other. The GROUP is on one or both sides, facing the thrones, their sides to the audience. They speak their lines to the audience.*

NARRATOR
We have a very sad story to tell you today. You've met Ahab. He was the *worst* king Israel ever had! He gave everyone headaches because he was *soooo* bad!

GROUP
(Holding their heads and looking back and forth to one another and the audience.) I hab and you hab an Ahab headache!

NARRATOR
He was so mean!

GROUP
I hab and you hab an Ahab headache!

NARRATOR
He was so dishonest!

GROUP

I hab and you hab an Ahab headache!

NARRATOR

And, boy! Was he ever greedy!

GROUP

I hab and you hab an Ahab headache!

JEZEBEL ENTERS and stands by AHAB.

NARRATOR

And if that wasn't bad enough, Ahab's wife was *even worse*! Her name was Jezebel, and she didn't like anyone! She didn't like the people of Israel. She didn't like Elijah the prophet. And she really didn't like God!

GROUP

(Holding their tummies and looking back and forth to one another and the audience) We have Jezebellyaches!

NARRATOR

She was meaner than Ahab.

GROUP

We have Jezebellyaches!

NARRATOR

She was more dishonest than Ahab.

GROUP

We have Jezebellyaches!

NARRATOR

And she was greedier than Ahab!

GROUP

We have Jezebellyaches!

NABOTH ENTERS, and stands to one side.

NARRATOR

Right next door to Ahab and Jezebel lived a man named Naboth.

NABOTH

(Holding his head and stomach) I hab a Ahab headache, *and* a Jezebellyache!

NARRATOR

Poor Naboth! He had a beautiful house, but …

NABOTH

I hab a Ahab headache, *and* a Jezebellyache!

NARRATOR

And he had a nice family, but …

NABOTH

I hab a Ahab headache, *and* a Jezebellyache!

NARRATOR

And he had a *wonderful* vineyard! But …

NABOTH

I hab a Ahab headache, *and* a Jezebellyache!

NARRATOR

What was the matter? (*AHAB walks over to NABOTH.*) I'll tell you what: Mean old king Ahab wanted Naboth's vineyard! He didn't want Naboth to have a nicer vineyard than his—he didn't want Naboth to have anything!

AHAB

I want that vineyard!

NARRATOR

Ahab didn't care that God says, "You shall not covet anything that is your neighbor's."

AHAB

I want that vineyard!

NARRATOR

Ahab tried to get Naboth to sell him the vineyard.

AHAB

I want that vineyard!

NARRATOR

But Naboth liked his vineyard. His father and grandfather had both lived there before him. He grew nice grapes and made good wine, and that was his job! He liked his house and his family and his vineyard, so Naboth wouldn't sell. So Ahab was very angry. He went home and pouted. (*AHAB returns to the throne and pouts. His arms are crossed and he has a long face.*)

JEZEBEL

What's wrong?

AHAB

I want that vineyard!

NARRATOR

Jezebel was very mean but also very smart. She had a plan!

JEZEBEL

I'll get the vineyard for you!

NARRATOR

So Jezebel wrote a letter to all the important people and said Naboth should be put on trial. Then she found two people to tell lies about Naboth.

LIARS come over to JEZEBEL. She whispers to them. They walk to NABOTH and point fingers at him.

NARRATOR

So the two liars made up bad things about Naboth.

GROUP

Liar, Liar, pants on fire!

NARRATOR

They said Naboth cursed God and King Ahab!

GROUP

Liar, Liar, pants on fire!

NARRATOR

They said Naboth should be killed!

GROUP

Liar, Liar, pants on fire!

AHAB and LIARS grab NABOTH and take him offstage.

NARRATOR

So Ahab and his friends took Naboth away from his home.

NABOTH

(Runs back on stage) I hab a Ahab headache *and* a Jezebellyache!

AHAB and LIARS grab NABOTH again and drag him offstage.

NARRATOR

And they killed poor Naboth! And they took his home and vineyard! And no one stopped them!

AHAB and JEZEBEL

(Jumping in victory) Yeah! We won!

NARRATOR

They didn't believe in the real God, and so they weren't sorry. They didn't ask to be forgiven. They thought they won!

GROUP

We hab Ahab headaches *and* Jezebellyaches! And we don't like that story! We like happy endings!

NARRATOR

I don't like it either, and sometimes mean people really do seem to win. *But* I have a little secret for you to remember: God knew all about Ahab and Jezebel—and eventually, Ahab and Jezebel had to answer to God. And then, Ahab and Jezebel had something worse than a headache, and worse than a bellyache. Meanwhile, poor Naboth, who lost his vineyard and even lost his life, had God's love and forgiveness—and a wonderful home in heaven! So, even this sad story has a happy ending after all! We have our own Ahab headaches and Jezebellyaches sometimes. But with God's love and forgiveness we'll also have a happy ending in heaven.

Nay, Nay, Naaman

∿∿∿∿∿∿∿

Text: 2 Kings 5:1–27

Level: Kindergarten–Primary

Participants: Narrator, Chorus, Naaman, Servant Girl, 1 Soldier, Elisha

Props: Boxes for a house; a sign that says "Elisha's House," another that says "Naaman's House;" child's bathing pool

Sound: Microphone for Narrator; lapel microphones for Naaman and Elisha

Setting the Stage: *CHORUS is off to one side. They need to do their lines vigorously, emphasizing the rhythm. The pool, if used, is down center, while the house is up center, labeled "Naaman's House." NAAMAN stands in front of it with the SERVANT GIRL, who is scrubbing. NAAMAN'S rhyming lines should be done in the manner of a childish temper tantrum.*

∿∿∿∿∿∿∿∿∿∿∿∿∿∿∿∿

NARRATOR

Long ago in a country far away called Aram, there lived a man named Naaman.

CHORUS

Naaman was a mighty man
An army man of the Aram land
Armed and very dangerous,
A soldier who was fabulous!

NARRATOR

A little girl from far away in the land of Israel had been taken to Aram. She worked for Naaman and his wife. She was honest and obedient, and they trusted her. Naaman became sick. (*NAAMAN pantomimes illness, holding his head and then itching and scratching his arms and legs.*) Even though he was still a big, strong soldier, he had a terrible disease called leprosy.

CHORUS

Naaman was a mighty man
An army man of the Aram land

Armed and very dangerous,
A soldier who was leperous.

NARRATOR

Naaman went to all the doctors in the land of Aram, but none could cure him. No one in Aram could help him. *(SERVANT GIRL stands up, pulls on NAAMAN'S arm and points offstage.)* But the little girl remembered a prophet named Elisha who lived in Israel, who had helped many people. She told Naaman that he should go to Israel to be healed. Naaman wasn't sure, but he thought maybe the Lord God of Israel could help him. His own gods sure hadn't helped. So Naaman traveled to Israel. *(NAAMAN EXITS with SERVANT GIRL. ELISHA ENTERS and changes the sign on the house to "Elisha's House." ELISHA sits by the house.)* When Naaman arrived in Israel, the king of Israel couldn't help him, but Elisha the prophet could. *(NAAMAN and one SOLDIER go to ELISHA's house. ELISHA and NAAMAN shake hands.)* So Naaman went to Elisha's house, hoping for a really impressive, superfantastic miracle. Elisha was God's prophet and he knew exactly what was wrong with Naaman. He also knew that God could help Naaman. So Elisha told Naaman what God had said:

ELISHA

(Pointing to the pool) Go wash yourself ...

NARRATOR

What, thought Naaman. He wanted some kind of exciting miracle, with Elisha waving his arms and saying magic words, but Elisha said he should go wash!?

NAAMAN

Nay, nay, nay! Nay I say:
I'll jump, I'll hop, I'll run, I'll walk
I'll pray and produce fancy talk
But I won't take a bath—no way!

ELISHA

(Pointing to the pool) Naaman, go wash yourself in the Jordan River.

NARRATOR

What, thought Naaman. Wash in the Jordan? That dirty, tiny, little river? What good would that do? Where was the excitement in that?

NAAMAN

Nay, nay, nay! Nay I say:
I'll work and slave and rant and rave
I'll do it all—I will behave,
But I won't take a bath today.

ELISHA

(Pointing to the pool) Go wash yourself in the Jordan River—seven times.

NARRATOR

Naaman thought Elisha was just crazy. What kind of miracle is there in washing—no matter how many times?!

NAAMAN

Nay, nay, nay! Nay I say:
I'll dip in a pool, I'll swim in a bay
I'll scrub in a tub, but there is no way
I'll take a Jordan bath today.

NARRATOR

Naaman was angry! And he was ready to go back home! Elisha was a useless prophet! Naaman turned around to go home. *(NAAMAN turns to leave. The SOLDIER stops him.)* But his servants stopped him.

CHORUS

Hey, hey, hey! Hey I say:
You'll dip in a pool, You'll swim in a bay
You'll scrub in a tub, but there is no way
You'll take a Jordan bath today? *(pause)*
What's the big deal?

NARRATOR

If God had told Naaman to take lots of medicine, he would have. If God told Naaman to do hard and difficult things, he would have. If God told Naaman to give lots of money, he would have.

NAAMAN

(Thoughtfully) Hmmmmmmmmm.

NARRATOR

And, after all, he was pretty sick! If he didn't get help soon, he would die!

CHORUS

Naaman was a mighty man
An army man of the Aram land
Armed and very dangerous,
Whose future was calamitous!

NARRATOR

Yep, he was facing a calamity. He would die if he didn't get help, and no one could help him. He'd tried everything and everybody … except God, the Lord God of Israel. So Naaman went to the Jordan River and washed seven times, just as Elisha had told him. … And he was healed! Just like that! God worked a great big miracle with a little bitty bath! And Naaman knew it! Even though he was raised to believe in other gods, now he knew there was only one real God—the God who healed him with a little bitty bath. (*NAAMAN, SOLDIER, and ELISHA all kneel together.*)

CHORUS

Naaman was a mighty man
An army man of the Aram land
Once he had been leperous
But then God made him just like us. *(pause)* Healthy!

NARRATOR

And you know what else? God has a miraculous bath for everyone, not just Naaman. It doesn't come from Elisha. It comes from Jesus, and it's called Baptism. Baptism washes away our sins and makes us God's children. It saves our lives—from death! All from a simple little bath! Nothing is too hard for God to do!

Ring around Jerusalem

Text: 2 Kings 18:1–19:37

Level: Preschool

Participants: Narrator, Hezekiah, Citizens of Jerusalem, Assyrians

Props: Boxes for Jerusalem; sign that says "Jerusalem"; crown; play money

Sound: Microphone for Narrator

Setting the Stage: *NARRATOR is at microphone; children are offstage.*

NARRATOR

After many, many bad kings—one right after another—the people of God in the land of Judah finally got a good king. His name was Hezekiah. Hezekiah trusted in God, and he obeyed everything God said. He got rid of all the idols in Judah, and he taught the people to worship the true God. God blessed him and the people of Judah in many ways. But not everything went well for Hezekiah. In a land far away, the King of Assyria had a mighty army. He sent his army to Judah to attack Jerusalem, where King Hezekiah lived.

ASSYRIANS

(Group marches in chanting) 1–2–3–4–1–2–3–4 *(stopping outside of Jerusalem).*

NARRATOR

King Hezekiah paid the king of Assyria all the money he had, hoping the army would go away. *(One SOLDIER comes forward; HEZEKIAH gives him play money.)* But the army didn't leave. Instead, they surrounded the whole city of Jerusalem, so no one could get out, and they told Hezekiah they were going to tear down the walls and kill everyone.

ASSYRIANS

(The ASSYRIANS join hands and make a circle around the city, skipping and singing to the tune of "Ring around the Rosie"— repeat at least twice.)
Ring around Jerusalem
It's lots and lots and lots of fun.
We're smashing, smashing the walls all down!

NARRATOR

Hezekiah was afraid, but he trusted that God would protect him and the people. But the Assyrian army was *very* strong and powerful!

ASSYRIANS

(Skipping and singing; repeat at least twice)
Ring around Jerusalem
It's lots and lots and lots of fun.
We're smashing, smashing the walls all down!

NARRATOR

The Assyrian army and their commander made fun of Hezekiah, and they made fun of the people of Judah. They even made fun of God! They told the people not to trust in the Lord. "He can't help you," they said. Hezekiah was really afraid, but he trusted in God, and he prayed and prayed for help. *(HEZEKIAH folds his hands.)*

CHORUS

(Skipping and singing; repeat at least twice)
Ring around Jerusalem
It's lots and lots and lots of fun.
We're smashing, smashing the walls all down!

NARRATOR

Things were looking pretty bad. The Assyrian army was big and powerful!

ASSYRIANS

(Cheering and shouting) Yeah! Yeah! Yeah!

NARRATOR

Judah's army was little and weak. *(HEZEKIAH and the people of Jerusalem look sad and scared.)*

ASSYRIANS

(Cheering and shouting) Yeah! Yeah! Yeah!

NARRATOR

The Assyrians had plenty of food and water.

ASSYRIANS

(Cheering and shouting) Yeah! Yeah! Yeah!

NARRATOR

The people of Jerusalem were starving.

ASSYRIANS

(Cheering and shouting) Yeah! Yeah! Yeah!

NARRATOR

It looked *very* bad!

ASSYRIANS

(Skipping and singing; repeat at least twice)
Ring around Jerusalem
It's lots and lots and lots of fun.
We're smashing, smashing the walls all down!

NARRATOR

But Hezekiah didn't give up. He prayed to God and said: "You are our Lord and our God! We ask You to keep us safe from the Assyrian king. Then everyone in every kingdom on earth will know that You are the only God." The Lord God heard Hezekiah's prayer and sent a prophet to promise that the Assyrians wouldn't tear down Jerusalem's walls. *(People in Jerusalem duck down beneath the walls.)* That very night, something amazing happened. *(ASSYRIANS fall over, one by one.)* All the Assyrian soldiers died! God sent an angel to punish them! When the people of Judah woke up and looked out, all the Assyrians were dead! God had rescued Hezekiah and the whole city!

JERUSALEM

Yeah! Yeah! Yeah!

NARRATOR

Hezekiah had a problem, and he prayed to God for help. When we have problems, we can pray to God and He will help us too.

ALL gather in a circle centerstage.

ALL

(Chanting) Praying to our God, the King,
We can praise, and we can sing.
God will help us with everything.

The B-I-B-L-E Is L-O-S-T

Text: 2 Kings 22:1–23:37

Level: Grades 3–6

Participants: Josiah, Shaphan, Hilkiah, 2 (or more) Idol Worshipers, Huldah, 2 (or more) Narrators

Props: Crown; T-shirt (that can be torn); throne for Josiah; drawing or statue (for an idol); boxes made into a building labeled "Temple"; Bible; chair for Huldah

Sound: Microphones for Narrators at opposite sides, lapel microphones for Josiah, Shaphan, Hilkiah, and Huldah (if possible)

Notes: *Have everyone, including the audience, sing parts marked SONG. Sing to the tune of the traditional children's song, "The B-I-B-L-E." Print out the different stanzas on poster board and have a student hold stanzas up for the audience to join in the singing.*

Setting the Stage: *Temple is up center—the boxes are disorganized, with one section falling down. "Idol" is stage left. A throne for JOSIAH is also stage left. HULDAH is sitting stage right.*

NARRATOR 2

The Bible tells us many things. It says that Jesus loves us. It tells us God made the world, and you and me too. It tells us all kinds of things that we need to know about what we should do and how we should live. It's a great book! What would we do without it?

SONG

The B-I-B-L-E
Was gone, L-O-S-T.
No one would look for the missing book,
The B-I-B-L-E.

NARRATOR 1

Yep, you heard it right. The Bible was missing, gone, L-O-S-T, lost. Back in the days when it was still being written, the people of Judah lost it! They just called it *the Law* back then, but whatever you call it, they lost it. During the time of Judah's bad kings, everyone—even the priests—forgot about God, and so they also forgot God's Word, the Bible, and lost it! L-O-S-T!

NARRATOR 2

Worst of all, no one noticed. No one cared. Everyone just did what they liked, and they believed almost anything, but not the Bible, 'cause it was L-O-S-T!

Two IDOL WORSHIPERS ENTER and bow down to the idol.

NARRATOR 1

They had their idols, and no one missed the Bible. But, after many years of rulers who didn't care at all about God, finally, a different kind of king was crowned. His name was Josiah.

JOSIAH ENTERS and sits down on his throne.

NARRATOR 2

Josiah wanted to serve God, but he didn't know much about how to do it. All around, people were worshiping idols, and Josiah didn't see any problem with that. But he did see another problem.

SHAPHAN ENTERS.

JOSIAH

Hey, Shaphan, look at the temple. It's falling down! Haven't we been collecting money to take care of it?

SHAPHAN

Yes, your majesty.

JOSIAH

Well, where's the money? Why isn't it fixed? Do we have any?

SHAPHAN

Yes, your majesty.

JOSIAH

Well, let's use it, then. Fix the temple!

SHAPHAN

Yes, your majesty.

SHAPHAN and HILKIAH fix the temple. HILKIAH "discovers" the Bible and pages through it.

NARRATOR 1

So they fixed up the temple. The high priest of the temple was named Hilkiah and, as they were fixing and cleaning the temple, he found a book.

HILKIAH

(Running to JOSIAH with SHAPHAN) Look what I found, your majesty.

JOSIAH

What is it?

SHAPHAN

It's called *the Law*—it's about God.

JOSIAH

Let me see that.

NARRATOR 2

Josiah read some things that worried him.

JOSIAH reads the Bible, getting a worried look.

JOSIAH

And God spoke all these words: "I am the LORD your God, who brought you out of Egypt, out of the land of slavery. You shall have no other gods before Me. You shall not make for yourself an idol in the form of anything in heaven above or on the earth beneath or in the waters below" *(Exodus 20:1–4)*.

SONG

The B-I-B-L-E
Is there for all to read
To hear, believe, and then obey
The B-I-B-L-E.

JOSIAH looks over at the idol worshipers.

JOSIAH

(JOSIAH rips his shirt. To SHAPHAN) Oh no! Idols! We've been worshiping idols—and lots of other things we're not supposed to do!

HILKIAH

Yes, your majesty.

JOSIAH

And it says here that God will punish His people for disobedience!

SHAPHAN

Yes, your majesty.

JOSIAH

And that we'll lose our land if we continue to disobey.

HILKIAH

Yes, your majesty.

JOSIAH

Is there anybody who can say anything besides, "Yes, your majesty"?

SHAPHAN/HILKIAH

(Pointing to HULDAH) Yes, your majesty. Try her!

NARRATOR 1

(JOSIAH crosses to HULDAH.) Josiah went to a prophet named Huldah. She was wise, and she knew the Lord.

JOSIAH

Look, we found the Bible. It says God will punish those who disobey. What are we going to do?

HULDAH

The Lord does punish, and He will punish Judah sooner or later for disobedience.

JOSIAH

Oh no!

HULDAH

But He would rather forgive. So He looks for repentance and faith, not perfection, where we have failed. It's part of His promise to us. He knows you are sorry—after all, you ripped your clothes. God will forgive you out of His mercy. Now try to obey what He says.

JOSIAH takes the Bible over to the idol worshipers and pantomimes reading to them. They get up and follow him to the temple.

NARRATOR 2

So Josiah and the people had another chance. They didn't lose the Bible again. Instead, they read it, and they followed it!

SONG

The B-I-B-L-E,
Yes, it's God's Word for me;
It tells me of His wondrous love,
The B-I-B-L-E.

Everything's Falling

Text: 2 Kings 23:1–25:28

Level: Grades 3–6

Participants: Narrator(s), Nebuchadnezzar and the Babylonians (five children or two thirds of the group if a large class); 5 Kings (optional—use crowns if there are not enough actors); Jerusalem Chorus (three to five very vocal kids, including the five kings, if used)

Props: Six paper crowns; throne; stacked boxes labeled "Jerusalem;" one poster board for each Babylonian; either with drawings of soldiers or with the word "thousands" printed in bold letters (poster boards are to be affixed to Babylonians' backs)

Sound: Microphone for Narrator(s)

Setting the Stage: *Boxes for Jerusalem are center, the throne is immediately downstage of the boxes with the crown on the seat of the throne. The JERUSALEM CHORUS is assembled around the throne.*

NARRATOR(S)

The kings of Israel and Judah were such a disappointment! There were 20 northern kings and 20 southern kings—and out of those 40 kings only eight were any good at all! Only eight even tried to serve the Lord! *(King or crown falls; replaced by another.)*

JERUSALEM CHORUS

(Sung to the tune of "When Johnny Comes Marching Home")
The kings are falling one by one, boo hoo, boo hoo.
The kings are falling one by one, boo hoo, boo hoo.
The kings are falling one by one,
Don't care about God in Jerusalem
And they all go falling down to the grave, where there's no one to save.
Boom, boom, boom!

NARRATOR

Some of the kings were bad, and others were just terrible! King Manasseh was one of the worst. He refused to worship God and he refused to treat the people right. He even burned little babies to death as sacrifices to false gods! He was *terrible!* Finally, he died. *(King or crown falls; replaced by another.)*

JERUSALEM CHORUS

The kings are falling one by one, boo hoo, boo hoo.
The kings are falling one by one, boo hoo, boo hoo.
The kings are falling one by one,
They cheat on their wives; they burn their sons;
And they all go falling down to the grave, where there's no one to save.
Boom, boom, boom!

NARRATOR

Other kings weren't much better. You remember lousy King Ahab and his rotten Queen Jezebel. But there were many other bad kings. One right after another. *(King or crown falls; replaced by another.)*

JERUSALEM CHORUS

The kings are falling one by one, boo hoo, boo hoo.
The kings are falling one by one, boo hoo, boo hoo.
The kings are falling one by one,
They lie and steal, and they think it's fun,
And they all go falling down to the grave, where there's no one to save.
Boom, boom, boom!

NARRATOR

King Josiah, who found the Bible, was the last good king of the people of God in Judah. Jehoahaz was the next king after Josiah. Although he was Josiah's son, he wasn't at all like his father. He refused to repent of his sins or turn to God. Thank goodness his kingdom didn't last long! *(King or crown falls; replaced by another.)*

JERUSALEM CHORUS

The kings are falling one by one, boo hoo, boo hoo.
The kings are falling one by one, boo hoo, boo hoo.
The kings are falling one by one,
They made life so bad in Jerusalem,
And they all went falling down to the grave, where there's no one to save.
Boom, boom, boom!

NARRATOR

After King Jehoahaz, along came King Jehoiakim. Like most of the other kings, he worshiped idols and paid no attention to God's Word. He raised the taxes and made the people pay and pay. The people were getting tired of all those kings, but so was God. He decided that enough was enough! A great and powerful king named Nebuchadnezzar of Babylon was forming a giant army, with thousands and thousands and thousands and thousands ... *(NEBUCHADNEZZAR, wearing the crown, and four BABYLONIANS ENTER, with the "thousands" posters fastened on their backs.)* Well, you get the picture, right? Anyway, there were so many soldiers you couldn't count them. King Jehoiakim could do nothing about an army so big ... he died too. *(King or crown falls; replaced by another.)*

JERUSALEM CHORUS

Babylon's coming a million to one, boo hoo, boo hoo.
Babylon's coming a million to one, boo hoo, boo hoo.
Babylon's coming a million to one,
Their army's surrounding Jerusalem,
While the people all go down to the grave, where there's no one to save.
Boom, boom, boom!

NARRATOR

Jehoiakim's son, Jehoiachin, became king, but only for three months. When the army of Babylon came to Jerusalem, Jehoiachin surrendered, paid Nebuchadnezzar all the money they had in Jerusalem, and the Babylonians took him away. Zedekiah became the king. You'd think he would have known better, but he ignored the Lord too, and he also made great king Nebuchadnezzar angry. *(Slowly and sadly)* You can guess what happened.

JERUSALEM CHORUS

(During the song, one box is removed for each line. During the last two lines, some of the people of Jerusalem fall dead.)
The walls are falling one by one, boo hoo, boo hoo.
The walls are falling one by one, boo hoo, boo hoo.
The walls are falling one by one,
This is the end of Jerusalem,
And the people all go down to the grave, where there's no one to save.
Boom, boom, boom! *(The BABYLONIANS march away.)*

NARRATOR

It was so sad. The kings all fell. Jerusalem fell. The temple fell. The people fell. Everything was destroyed. People were killed. Others were taken to Babylon as slaves. It was a sad, sad time. And it happened because the kings and the people wouldn't listen. They wouldn't repent—they wouldn't turn away from their sins. So they all went down to the grave. *(The JERUSALEM CHORUS falls over, dead.)*

NARRATOR

But the song was wrong! There is someone to save, even from the grave! Many years later, a new king came to Jerusalem. His name was Jesus. He didn't come with an army, but He has saved a whole army of followers—people from long ago and people from today who trust in His love. He is the real King they needed long ago and the only one we need today. He's the King who rose from the grave. He's the King who comes to save.

ALL

(Very loudly) The King has come, and He's the one, hurrah! Hurrah!
The King has come, and He's the one, hurrah! Hurrah!
The King has come, He's the only One,
The King of the world and Jerusalem,
And He even went on down to the grave, to be able to save
Ev'ryone, *(Shout)* Yes!

A Test for Esther

Text: Esther 1:1–10:3

Level: Grades 3–6

Participants: Narrator(s), King Ahasuerus-Xerxes, Mordecai, Haman, Group (4–7 children), Servant, Esther

Props: Table and chairs; plates and at least one goblet; chair for throne; scroll (paper towel holder wrapped with white paper); sword and scepter; tall stepladder; rope shaped in a noose

Sound: Microphones for the Narrators, Xerxes, Haman, Mordecai, and Esther

Setting the Stage: *The opening scene has XERXES and the group seated at a table, feasting. The group includes MORDECAI and HAMAN. MORDECAI claps for the king, but does not join in the group's lines in the opening scene. A SERVANT is standing at attention off to one side.*

NARRATOR(S)

Long ago, the people of Judea were taken away to a foreign land. While they were far from home, there came a new king. The king's name was Xerxes, or Ahasuerus, and his queen was Vashti. They lived in the city of Susa. Ahasuerus was so powerful that everyone wanted to be his friend, and most people told him whatever he wanted to hear. He had many, many advisors—important people who were supposed to help the king. One of them was …

MORDECAI

(Turning toward audience) Mordecai. I'm one of the foreigners from Judea, which makes me a Jew. I've tried to help the king, Ahasuerus, also known as Xerxes, in every way that I can, though he seldom notices.

NARRATOR

Another advisor was named …

HAMAN

(Turning toward audience) Haman! And *I* intend to be the king's favorite. I'm smarter than he is anyway, and soon I'll have him doing what *I* say!

NARRATOR

Xerxes wasn't a terrible king, but he was kind of foolish because he was such a show off. He wanted everyone to tell him how important he was—and, as kings tend to do, he demanded that everybody do exactly what he said all the time.

The following lines are sung to the tune of "Let's Go Fly a Kite" from Mary Poppins. *Or, these lines can be spoken rhythmically.*

XERXES

I am Ahasuerus.

GROUP

You're simply marvelous!

XERXES

Xerxes is my other name.

GROUP

Either way, your fame's the same.

XERXES

I am the very best!

GROUP

So far beyond the rest!

XERXES

I am the number one king.
I serve the best of things!
Food that's fit for queens or kings!
I drink the finest wines!
From rich, expensive vines!
I am Ahasuerus.

GROUP

You're simply marvelous!

XERXES

I am the number one king.
And I, ...

GROUP

You!

XERXES

I, simply marvelous Ahasuerus, ... I, who have only the best, because I am the best ... I have the most beautiful wife in the world—bring her out here!

GROUP

(Cheering) Vashti! Vashti! Bring on Vashti!

The SERVANT turns and beckons offstage, first in a dignified way, then becoming more and more frantic, until he finally turns back, looking nervous.

SERVANT

Um, er, uh, well, uh, I think she's busy.

GROUP

(To one another) Uh oh!

XERXES

(Angrily) She *what*?

GROUP

Uh oh!!

XERXES

No one is *ever* too busy for me! Get her *now*!

The SERVANT turns again, beckoning offstage more and more frantically. Again, he turns back nervously.

XERXES

Well???

SERVANT

Uh, um, um, um.

GROUP

Uh oh!!

XERXES

Well???

SERVANT

(Ducking as he speaks) She says she won't come out.

GROUP

UH OHHHHH!!!

XERXES

(Standing) She—WON'T—come?

SERVANT

(Cringing) No, she won't. I'm sorry.

GROUP

(Spoken by separate individuals from the group) Now what? Let her have it! Don't let a woman push you around! Teach her a lesson!

GROUP EXITS, taking the table and dishes. XERXES moves to the throne and sits, meditatively.

NARRATOR

Well, Xerxes did something all right. He made Vashti give up her crown—she was no longer the queen. He kicked her right out! Poor Vashti. But now he had no queen. Everyone knows a king needs a queen, so he decided he'd get an even more beautiful queen than before. *(XERXES holds up one finger.)* He sent messengers everywhere to find beautiful young women. He would choose the one he liked the best. The messengers went all through the land and found hundreds of beautiful young women. One beautiful woman didn't live far away. She was practically next door to the king, living with her uncle Mordecai, a wise man who often gave advice to the king.

MORDECAI and ESTHER enter from one side.

NARRATOR

Mordecai's niece was also wise. Her name was Esther. She was wise, *and* she was beautiful. And … she was taken to see Xerxes.

SERVANT ENTERS opposite MORDECAI and ESTHER, sees ESTHER, and leads her to XERXES.

XERXES

What is *your* name?

ESTHER

Esther.

XERXES

(To SERVANT) She is just what I've been looking for! Meet my new queen! *(ESTHER sits down beside the king in a lower chair. SERVANT stands on the other side.)*

NARRATOR

So Esther became the queen. She was rich and famous! But she was also afraid—afraid to do anything that might make Xerxes angry. Meanwhile, Mordecai was so wise that he discovered some people who were trying to kill the king. He told Esther and Esther told Xerxes about the plot. Xerxes punished the murderers and his life was spared.

Even though Mordecai had saved the king's life, the King liked Haman the best of all his advisors. Haman was constantly telling Xerxes how wonderful he was.

HAMAN

O king, you are the greatest.

XERXES

(Smugly) Yes, I am.

HAMAN

It is a privilege to serve you, O marvelous Ahasuerus!

XERXES

I'm sure it is!

HAMAN

It's an honor to give you gifts. You are soooooooooooo wonderful.

XERXES

Yes, it's true! Say, you really are brilliant, aren't you!

HAMAN

Whatever you say, O King!

XERXES

Perceptive!

HAMAN

You know all, O King!

XERXES

Positively astute!

HAMAN

King, your wisdom exceeds description!

XERXES

Indeed! *(To SERVANT)* Call all my advisors immediately!

SERVANT runs off and returns immediately with GROUP.

XERXES

Because Haman is so brilliant, I am hereby giving him the title *Favorite of Xerxes*!

GROUP

Long live Haman, favorite of Xerxes. *(Everyone except MORDECAI bows down before HAMAN. HAMAN smiles proudly at everyone individually until he notices MORDECAI. He stops and glares.)*

SERVANT

(To MORDECAI) You'd better bow down, Mordecai. … You'll get in trouble! … Why won't you bow? Everyone else is!

MORDECAI

I am a Jew.

GROUP EXITS with ESTHER. Only XERXES, HAMAN, and SERVANT remain.

NARRATOR

Haman noticed that Mordecai would not bow down before him. Mordecai worshiped no man or woman, for his people believed in and worshiped only the one true Ruler of all the world. But the servant was right. Mordecai was in trouble. For now Haman hated him.

HAMAN

O wonderful King, did you know you have a whole group of people in your kingdom who are making trouble?

XERXES

(Shocked) What? Who are they?

HAMAN

The Jews, O King. They're awful. They're evil. They're terrible.

XERXES

I won't have it! This must be stopped!

HAMAN

They all hate you! They refuse to bow down before you and worship your majesty!

XERXES

But … I am Ahasuerus!

HAMAN

(Cheering) You're simply marvelous!

XERXES

Xerxes is my other name.

HAMAN

Either way, the fame's the same.

XERXES

I am the very best!

HAMAN

(Cheering) So far beyond the rest.

XERXES

(Lifting his plate) I serve the best of things!

HAMAN

(Cheering) The kind that's fit for kings!

XERXES

(Lifting his goblet) I drink the finest wines!

HAMAN

(Cheering) From rich, expensive vines!

XERXES

(Waving toward SERVANT) And I ...

HAMAN

You!

XERXES

I ... I ... I won't have it!

HAMAN

No sir!

XERXES

This must stop!

HAMAN

They must be punished!

XERXES

I'll ...

HAMAN

You'll ...

XERXES

I'll ...

HAMAN

You'll …

XERXES

I'll …

HAMAN

If you like, *I'll* take care of it!

XERXES

This sounds expensive!

HAMAN

I'll take care of it, *and* I'll pay for it.

XERXES

Wonderful, just sign my name.

HAMAN

Your wish is my command. I'll take care of those scoundrels.

XERXES and SERVANT EXIT to one side. HAMAN skips out the other, gleefully.

NARRATOR

So Haman wrote an order, with Ahasuerus' seal, that at the end of the year, all in one day, on Friday the 13th, all the Jews would be killed! Mordecai heard about the decree. He knew that soon he and all his people would die. He cried and prayed—he was worried! Esther saw how worried he was.

ESTHER and MORDECAI ENTER, MORDECAI carrying a scroll.

ESTHER

What's wrong, Mordecai?

MORDECAI

(Handing her the scroll) We're dead. We'll all be killed. See!

ESTHER

(Reading) All the Jews to be killed?

MORDECAI

You're the only one who can stop it, Esther. You are the queen!

ESTHER

But he's the king! If I even walk into the room without permission, he can kill me!

MORDECAI

But if you don't try, we will all be killed!

ESTHER

I'm afraid!

MORDECAI

Esther, you are also a Jew.

ESTHER

(After a long pause) Mordecai, tell everyone to fast and pray.

Song option: Sing "Make Me a Servant," by Kelly Willard.

ESTHER and MORDECAI EXIT. XERXES returns to the throne with HAMAN and SERVANT beside him. ESTHER ENTERS from behind the audience, waiting in the back until summoned.

NARRATOR

After three days of prayerful fasting, Esther went to the king. What would he do? *(XERXES and HAMAN look up.)* He hadn't asked her to come. *(XERXES stands. HAMAN picks up a sword.)* If he didn't want to see her, she would be killed! *(XERXES puts his hands on his hips, staring. HAMAN reaches with the sword, trying to hand it to XERXES.)*

SERVANT

An unannounced visitor, O King.

XERXES

What? Who is that coming to bother me without permission? ... Is that you, Esther? *(ESTHER nods nervously. XERXES reaches for the scepter from SERVANT and extends it toward ESTHER, smiling.)* Come on up to my throne! *(HAMAN pouts and puts down the sword.)*

ESTHER

Thank you, O King, but I only wanted to invite you and Haman to dinner tomorrow.

XERXES smiles. HAMAN looks overjoyed.

XERXES

We'll be happy to come. In return, I shall give you anything you ask!

XERXES, HAMAN, SERVANT, and ESTHER all EXIT. As the NARRATOR speaks the following lines, a table and chairs are set up with plates and goblets.

NARRATOR

So Esther prepared a feast fit for a king. Haman went home, thrilled that he, favorite of Xerxes, was the only advisor included in Esther's party. The only problem was that he saw Mordecai on the way home and—again—Mordecai refused to bow down before him. Grrrrrrr! That made him so angry!

HAMAN ENTERS with GROUP.

HAMAN

I have good news, and I have bad news!

GROUP

Tell us!

HAMAN

The good news is that *I*, Haman, am the only person Queen Esther invited to a banquet for the king tomorrow!

GROUP

Yeah!

HAMAN

(Pouting) The bad news is that *I*, Haman, friend of Xerxes, most important advisor in all the land, walked by Mordecai, the *Jew*, the rat, the *nobody*, on my way home and he refused to bow to me *again*! I hate him! I can't wait until we get to kill the Jews.

FEMALE

(A female member of GROUP) I know what you need to be happy!

HAMAN

(Whining) Nothing will make me happy!

FEMALE

Why don't you build a gallows tonight?

HAMAN

I'm tired. I don't want to build anything!

FEMALE

Build the gallows that you will use to hang Mordecai on Friday the 13th!

HAMAN

(Going from a pout to a mean smile) You know what, I *like* that idea! Get my hammer!

GROUP EXITS. HAMAN returns immediately with the ladder, with a noose hanging down, setting it up upstage. HAMAN EXITS. XERXES and SERVANT ENTER, SERVANT carrying a scroll. XERXES paces, SERVANT follows him.

NARRATOR

A funny thing happened on the way to the banquet. It started the night before. Xerxes couldn't sleep, so he asked his servant to read to him about all the things that he had done since he became king. While the servant was reading, he read about the time that Mordecai had saved Xerxes' life. Xerxes had forgotten, of course, but now that he was reminded, he made up his mind to reward Mordecai immediately. He needed Haman's advice!

HAMAN

(Knocking) O King?

XERXES

Just the man I wanted to see!

HAMAN

(Proudly) Yes, I wanted to tell you I built a ...

XERXES

Not now! Listen, what should I do for the best advisor I've ever had?

NARRATOR

Well, now! Haman knew who that was! Or he thought he did.

HAMAN

(Cupping his hand and whispering to SERVANT) That's got to mean me!!! Oh, boy! *(To XERXES)* I think you should give that person wonderful presents and let him ride your own horse through town. Oh, and have the second best advisor lead the horse for him, that way everyone will know who the *best* advisor is!

XERXES

That is brilliant, Haman! I love it. Now, go get some beautiful jewels ...

HAMAN

(Greedily) Yes!

XERXES

And get some gold—a whole lot!

HAMAN

(Rubbing his hands) Yes!!

XERXES

And get my horse!

HAMAN

Of course!

XERXES

And then, give all the presents to Mordecai, and put him on the horse, and lead him around through town! ... Then meet me at Esther's for the banquet!

SERVANT and XERXES—looking pleased with himself—EXIT. HAMAN remains, looking shocked.

HAMAN

(Stunned, as he EXITS, opposite side) Jewels!? ... Gold!? ... The king's horse!? ... For Mordecai!? *(Pulling his hair)* Aaaaaaaahhhhhh!!!

A table and chairs are set up down center, with the king's "throne" and the plate and goblet placed at the head of the table.

NARRATOR

So Haman was humiliated, but his problems were just starting. Later, he and Xerxes went to Esther's house for her banquet.

ESTHER ENTERS first, carrying a dish to the table. Then, HAMAN and XERXES ENTER. HAMAN is pouting.

XERXES

What a feast! Wonderful, don't you think so, Haman?

HAMAN

(Mumbling) Sure ... fine.

XERXES

Don't know what's wrong with you today! But anyway, my Queen, you have prepared such a wonderful feast that I must do something wonderful in return! Name it! What would you like? Diamonds?

Song option: Sing the following to the tune of "O Lord, Won't You Buy Me a Mercedes Benz" by Janis Joplin.

> O Queen, can I buy you a chariot Benz?
> Your friends all have horses, I must make amends.
> You've worked hard in the kitchen, no help from your friends.
> O Queen, can I buy you a chariot Benz?
>
> O Queen, can I buy you a new jeweled crown?
> You look kinda sad, dear, what has got you down?
> I like you far better in a smile than a frown,
> O Queen, can I buy you a new jeweled crown?
>
> O Queen, can I buy you a palace of gold?
> Your house needs a painting, the furniture's old.
> Just pick what you want and the property's sold,
> O Queen, can I buy you a palace of gold?

ESTHER

I want only one thing, O King, O Ahasuerus, O Xerxes.

XERXES

(Proudly) Anything! I am Ahasuerus. I'm simply marvelous! Xerxes is my other name. Either way, the fame's the same. I am the very best! So far beyond the rest. I serve the best of things! The kind that's fit for kings! I drink the finest wines! From rich, expensive vines! And I will give you anything! Jewels, gold, horses, houses, anything!

ESTHER

I would like you to spare my life.

XERXES

(Shocked) Huh?

ESTHER

Yes, I would like to live.

XERXES

I don't get it.

ESTHER

I am a Jew, O King, and a decree has gone out from you that all the Jews are to be killed at the end of this year, on Friday the 13th.

HAMAN looks shocked and starts to cringe.

XERXES

What? I never!

ESTHER hands him the scroll.

XERXES

What is this? ... *(Very angry, turning around slowly toward HAMAN.)* Who did this? Haman? My *favorite*?

HAMAN scurries around to ESTHER and falls down in front of her, grabbing her around the waist.

XERXES

And now you're grabbing my *wife*!

HAMAN lets go and starts to run offstage, the king chasing him. ESTHER EXITS on the other side.

HAMAN

Help! Help! Help! I'll never be bad again!

NARRATOR

But it was too late for Haman to change. That very day the king had him hanged from the gallows he had made for Mordecai. Then the king sent a new edict to all the land, threatening death to anyone who tried to harm the Jews. And, on Friday the 13th, the day Haman wanted the Jews to be killed, their enemies were defeated instead. And the next day, the 14th, the Jews rested and celebrated together. So Xerxes, perhaps, learned a lesson about real friends. And Esther was the hero of her people, and Mordecai was a hero for his people. But there was one other hero: the One who wasn't even named. The One who made Mordecai wise and made Esther brave—the One who saved His people, the Jews. The One all the Jewish people thank in a celebration called Purim on the 14th day of the last month of the year.

Exiles

Texts: The books of Ezra, Nehemiah, and Haggai

Level: Grades 4–6

Participants: Narrator(s), Cyrus, five or more (preferably more) people of Judah including Zerubbabel, Jeshua, Haggai, Ezra, and Nehemiah; a Group of Enemies.

Props: Bible costuming if desired; empty boxes to represent stones; a large piece of cardboard labeled "Temple"; placards that say: "Boo!" "Go Home!" "Down with Judah!" or similar things—one for each enemy.

Sound: Microphones for the Narrators; either tape or piano accompaniment to Linda Ronstadt's "So Far Away"

Setting the Stage: *NARRATORS are at microphones on either side of the stage. The PEOPLE OF JUDAH are gathered centerstage.*

NARRATOR 1

586 years before Christ, King Nebuchadnezzar destroyed Jerusalem and took many people off to Babylon. People like Daniel and Esther lived in foreign lands for a long, long time. They were in exile. They were homesick for their own land of Judah and the city of Jerusalem.

(Sung to the tune of Linda Ronstadt's "So Far Away.")

JUDAH

We are so far away,
No one really owns their own place anymore.
It would be so fine to open my own front door,
Go home and there to stay,
But we're so far away.

So far away,
Living in a land where it all seems so strange.
I don't speak their language, and I don't play their games.
Sadness for every day,
'Cause we're so far away.

NEHEMIAH

(Spoken) We've been here forever.

EZRA

I'm homesick.

ZERUBBABEL

I wish there was something we could do to get home.

NEHEMIAH

Maybe we could sneak away?

EZRA

Maybe we could stow away?

HAGGAI

(Sarcastically) Sure, and maybe we could fly away!

JESHUA

But, we really *could* pray.

JUDAH

(Sung to the tune of "So Far Away")
When there is just no way,
No way that you know how to get through your day.
There's still one thing to remember—one thing more I can say.
Now is the time to pray—
Yes, you can always say:
(Spoken) **The Lord is good and His love endures forever!**

PEOPLE OF JUDAH EXIT.

NARRATOR 2

After 70 years of praying, God made a way for His people in exile to come home. A king named Cyrus understood that the people of Judah should go home to Jerusalem and rebuild the temple.

CYRUS speaks from offstage; while he speaks, boxes are strewn around centerstage.

CYRUS

" 'The LORD, the God of heaven, has given me all the kingdoms of the earth and He has appointed me to build a temple for Him at Jerusalem in Judah. Anyone of His people among you—may his God be with him, and let him go up to Jerusalem in Judah and build the temple of the LORD, the God of Israel, the God who is in Jerusalem' " (*Ezra 1:2–3*).

NARRATOR 1

It seemed simple enough: The people could go home and rebuild God's temple, and Cyrus would even help pay for it. The leaders of the people of Judah were Zerubbabel and Jeshua.

A group of three or more (including ZERUBBABEL, JESHUA, and HAGGAI) comes slowly up the center aisle to the stage. Halfway up the aisle, ZERUBBABEL and JESHUA speak.

ZERUBBABEL

This is so cool! We finally get to go home to Jerusalem and see everything all the old people told us about!

JESHUA

I can't wait to see it!

NARRATOR 2

So Zerubbabel and Jeshua and the first group of people came home to Jerusalem. They were used to living in Babylon and Persia in beautiful rich cities and towns with lots of food and nice homes. Were they ever surprised to see Jerusalem!

The GROUP arrives centerstage.

JESHUA

This place is a mess! Everything is torn down!

ZERUBBABEL

Where will we live? What will we eat? Where will we get clothes?

NARRATOR 1

It was pretty discouraging. There was so much to do. There were no homes. No walls. No stores. They had so much to do they decided to …

JESHUA

Pray! We'll never do it all! We need to pray!

ZERUBBABEL

Pray?

JUDAH

(Sung to the tune of "So Far Away")
When there is just no way,
No way that you'll get all your work done today.
When all you see is trouble and there's no time to play,
Then fall down t' your knees
'Cause now it's time to pray!
(Spoken) **The Lord is good and His love endures forever!**

PEOPLE OF JUDAH begin to gather and stack the boxes.

NARRATOR 2

Then the people started to build homes and places for their families. It was hard work.
It cost a lot of money. But, somehow, they got it done and built homes and towns. But
the temple wasn't even started. So God sent the prophet Haggai to Zerubbabel.

HAGGAI

God says we're forgetting something.

ZERUBBABEL

What?

HAGGAI

The temple.

ZERUBBABEL

Oh no! It's going to be hard to build the temple. It's going to cost a lot. It will take even
more money. And our enemies don't want it built. Where will we start? Maybe we
should take a collection. Maybe we should hire soldiers. Maybe we should …

HAGGAI

Pray!

JUDAH

(Sung to the tune of "So Far Away")
When there is just no way,
No way that you'll get all your work done today.
When all you see is trouble and there's no time to play,
Then fall down t' your knees
'Cause now it's time to pray!
(Spoken) **The Lord is good and His love endures forever!**

NARRATOR 1

So they gave sacrifices and prayed at the altar of the ruined temple. And then they
worked and worked and prayed and prayed and built and built. And finally, the temple
was done! But more people were coming all the time. And there were enemies too. Lots
of them. Powerful ones. They didn't want all the people coming back to Jerusalem.

*Cardboard "temple" has been erected. The rest of Judah join the center group, including
NEHEMIAH and EZRA. GROUP OF ENEMIES carrying signs ENTERS and stands
upstage in a semicircle around the people of Judah.*

NARRATOR 2

The people were afraid. Their enemies made trouble. They made Judah's life miserable!
They had to stop the enemies. They needed swords and soldiers and armies. They needed to …

NEHEMIAH

Pray!

JUDAH

(Sung to the tune of "So Far Away")
When there is just no way,
No way that you'll get all your work done today.
When all you see is trouble and there's no time to play,
Then fall down t' your knees
'Cause now it's time to pray!
(Spoken) **The Lord is good and His love endures forever!**

NARRATOR 1

And God sent Nehemiah. They prayed and prayed. And Nehemiah organized the people into teams. They built with one hand and held their swords in the other. And the enemies stayed away! So the city was safe. There were homes. There was a temple. And there were walls. Now they could rest, so they all gathered to listen to Ezra read the Bible and then …

EZRA

Pray!

JUDAH

(Sung to the tune of "So Far Away")
So when your work's all done,
You've finally arrived at the end of the day.
Finally time to rest 'cause now you're at home to stay.
Then back onto your knees
'Cause it's still time to pray.
(Spoken) **The Lord is good and His love endures forever!**

Surfin' Galilay

Text: Matthew 8:23–33

Level: Grades 4–6

Participants: 12 disciples (including Peter), Jesus, person to portray the storm

Props: Small benches for disciples, two longer benches stacked on their sides to look like a boat; a pole with a sheet to look like a sail; box fan; and extension cord

Lights: Spotlights for boat and Jesus are desirable but not necessary

Sound: Lapel microphones for Peter and Jesus

Setting the Stage: *Some sort of mock boat is centerstage—the simpler the better. A mast of some sort is desirable. The DISCIPLES are in the boat singing—their song is sung to the tune of the Beach Boys' "Till Daddy Takes the T-Bird Away."*

12

Well, we're the 12 dude disciples
And we're crossing this big old lake now!
Seems we forgot all about the things
Jesus use'ta say now.
So with all the wind blastin'
We'll go cruisin' just as fast as we can now!
And we'll have fun, fun, fun,
'Til Big Daddy takes the sunshine away!

WIND person carries in a box fan. If the person talks right into the back of the fan it makes strange noises. WIND can wear a sign that says "Big Bad Storm."

12

(Ad libbing complaints about how tough life is ... nothing ever goes right ... bickering and fussing, etc. Increasing panic ending with the sail being ripped down. Finally) We're gonna drown!

Singing continues.

Well, we knew all along
That Big Daddy was wise to you now! *(Pointing accusingly at each other)*
Now He's ripped off the sail
And there's nothing that we can do now.
So we're in mighty big trouble,
And I think we're all gonna drown now!
Well, we had fun, fun, fun,
'Til Big Daddy took the sunshine away!

JESUS ENTERS from the aisle, singing and dancing. He sings to the tune of the Beach Boys' "I Get Around."

JESUS

Get around, get around, I get around.
Get around, round, round! I get around!
Whoa, I get around. I get around! Yo, I get around.

DISCIPLE 1

Dude … check out the *surfer*!

DISCIPLE 2

Yo, Dude … that's a Surfin Spirit!

Yikes … a *ghost*!

JESUS

(Surfing up to the boat, speaks in Valley talk) Chill out, dudes! I'm a ghost? … As if … It's like … me! Relax!

PETER

Hey, Dude … can I do that? Please, please? Can I? Can I?

JESUS

Whatever. *(To the crowd)* Like I wonder if he remembers his name means *rock*?

PETER

(Walking on the water, singing to the tune of "Surfin' USA")
If everybody had faith, dude, across Galilay
Then everybody'd be surfin', like I am today!
All you need's a little faith now,
And you can do it too!
(starts looking around in panic) Whoa these waves are gettin' big now
(shouting and falling to the floor) **I think I'm gonna drown!**

JESUS rolls His eyes, moves toward PETER.

PETER

(Singing to the tune of "Help Me, Rhonda")
Help me, Jesus, help, help me, Jesus.
Help me, Jesus, help, help me, Jesus.

JESUS

(Lifting PETER up and dropping him in the boat) Your faith is like so small, man! What is with all of you?

DISCIPLE 1

We forget, Dude! But, like, wow, that was like awesome that You saved him anyway, even when he was doubting and drowning! You're like God Himself, Man!

Singing continues.

12

If everybody had faith, dude, across Galilay
Then everybody'd be surfin', like we are today!
All you need is some faith now, And you can do it too!
Though the waves will be kickin', Jesus always comes through!

Nick at Night

Text: John 3:1–16

Level: Grades 4–8

Participants: Narrator, Chorus, Nicodemus, Jesus

Props: Bed (bench); door or curtain; chair

Sound: Microphone for Narrator, Jesus, and Nicodemus

Setting the Stage: *A simple set with the bed in the center and a chair nearby. A doorway of some sort (a curtain will do) is to one side. JESUS is sleeping. The CHORUS and NARRATOR can either be off to the side or they can ENTER, standing down center, in front of JESUS. The song is to the tune of "In the Still of the Night." Boys do the last line alone.*

CHORUS

In the dark of the night,
Somebody's stumblin' to the light.
He is lost. He's so alone.
He is so far, so far from home
In the dark of the night. *(Boys)* It's Nick at night.

NARRATOR

Late one night while Jesus was sleeping, there came a knick … er, I mean, a *knock* at the door.

Loud knocking sound awakens JESUS.

JESUS

Yes? Come in, Nick.

NICODEMUS

(Sticks his head in the door. Starting in, he stops.) Wait! How'd You know it was me, Jesus? *(ENTERS)* Wow—just add one more thing to the list of ways You amaze me.

JESUS

Sit down, Nicodemus.

NICODEMUS

I gotta talk to You, Jesus.

NARRATOR

Nicodemus had heard about the things Jesus did—like healing the sick or turning water into wine.

NICODEMUS

You're awesome, man! But I'm in the dark. I'm …

JESUS

… you're confused?

NARRATOR

How could Jesus do all those things? Nick was in the dark. The only thing he knew was that it had something to do with God.

NICODEMUS

I know God is with You somehow, like You must be like some prophet or something. But I'm still in the dark.

JESUS

That's because to really get what God's power is about, you have to be born again.

NICODEMUS

(Sarcastically) Born again? … yeah, right!

JESUS

Yes, born again.

NICODEMUS

Sure! Born again! (Falls on the floor laughing hysterically.)

JESUS

(Pauses, looking, then) Nick?

NICODEMUS

(Still laughing, but trying to stop as he sees that JESUS is serious) You're not kidding?

JESUS shakes His head no, looking calmly at NICODEMUS.

NICODEMUS

Uh, do you see a size problem here, Jesus? *(Scrunching down)* Like I'm gonna get real little and go back into Mom again? *(Jumping up)* No, I get it—I know where I'll fit. I'll be born again as an elephant! *(Marches around and mimics an elephant waving its trunk)* No, maybe a rhino ... that'd be real pleasant! *(Lowers his head and paws the ground)* Or, how about ...

JESUS

Nick!

NICODEMUS stops.

JESUS

No one enters God's kingdom unless he's born of water and the Spirit.

NICODEMUS

Oh, that's great. Water! *(Mimes swimming)* Now I understand—I do a Jonah. *(Singing)* "Under the sea ... under the sea ..." I'd definitely fit inside a whale! *(Singing)* "Splish, splash, I was takin' a bath ..." when ... GULP! Rebirth, here I come!

JESUS

Nick ... please. Human beings have human babies, right? Flesh gives birth to flesh. But if you want to connect with God, you have to be born from GOD: Spirit gives birth to spirit. So you have to be born again, born from above.

NICODEMUS

Hey, man! Born *from above!* Rocket man! Beam me down, Scotty! ... Captain Kirk ... or maybe "Captain Jesus" ... this does not compute!

JESUS

I get it, Spock, right?

NARRATOR

Nick was really in the dark. He wanted everything to make sense. But he was forgetting that God can do more than we can understand.

CHORUS

(Singing) In the dark of the night,
Nick is movin' away from the light.
It is dark; he is blind.
True understanding is so hard to find,
In the dark of the night. *(Boys)* It's Nick at night.

NARRATOR

So what will he do? Will he listen and believe, or will he have to understand everything before he accepts what Jesus is saying?

NICODEMUS

(Pauses, thinking, then sits down.) All right. I'm sorry. Go on. I'll listen.

JESUS

Good. Please believe what I'm saying to you. And you know I turned water into wine?

NICODEMUS

(Nodding his head) Yeah, I know about that.

JESUS

Nick, I can do more. I can change you. I can make you new.

NICODEMUS

But what does water have to do with it?

JESUS

When the Spirit gets into it, water can give you a whole new life.

NICODEMUS

Spirit? Now You're talking about ghosts? I'm really in the dark!

JESUS

No, I am talking about *a* Ghost, a Holy Ghost—the Holy Spirit. You can't see Him, but He's there when My words are used with water. You'll know He's there because lives will change.

NICODEMUS

I don't know if I can believe that.

JESUS

That's the question all right.

NICODEMUS

What?

JESUS

Do you believe Me? That's the bottom line, Nick. That's the only way out of the dark. Just believe Me, Nick, and see what I do with water and words. You will be born again.

JESUS puts His arm around NICODEMUS.

CHORUS

In the dark of the night,
Jesus is shining. Jesus is Light.
He's the way, the truth, the life.
He ends the darkness, He ends the strife
In the dark of the night. *(Boys)* The end, "Amen."

Rockball, Our Natural Pastime

Text: John 8:1–11

Level: Grades 4–6

Participants: Announcer, Zebedee MacGee, Woman, JesusUmp, as many rock throwers as desired

Props: Chair and microphone for Zebedee; home plate; wall backdrop; Wiffle balls; baseball gloves and caps; uniforms if possible

Lighting: Spotlight on Woman and JesusUmp if possible.

Sounds: Microphone for Zebedee, lapel microphone for Jesus and rock throwers if possible.

Setting the Stage: *Scene involves a woman against a wall. Home plate is right in front of her. JesusUmp is dressed in umpire gear. As many pitchers as are available are dressed in baseball uniforms with ball gloves; all but the starter are seated on a bench. ANNOUNCER is seated at a table to the side or above the bench with a microphone. If many kids are available, they can be fans cheering or in bleachers. ANNOUNCER is best played by an adult with a Harry Caray announcer voice.*

ANNOUNCER

Hello, sports fans … My name is Zebedee MacGee and I wanna welcome you to the temple gates of Jerusalem. We're at the gate Beautiful, and it is a BEYOOTIFUL day for ROCKBALL! Today's game pits the hometown Pharisee Flamethrowers against One Naughty Woman! As you know, sports fans, in rockball it's either all offense or all defense. The offense gets to pitch stones at the defense until the defense gets spattered all over the town wall! What a great game, huh, sports fans! No suspense and the home team always wins!!! Besides, don't you love them odds … 10 *(or however many pitchers will be used)* fire-breathing, stone throwing Pharisees against one helpless whimpering woman!!! YA GOTTA LOVE THIS GAME! 'Course, today we are gonna do one thing different. Somebody came up with the idea of having uh, uh, whadda they call it? Oh, yeah, an *Umpire* … so let me introduce today's ump, a guy named Jesus! They picked Him because He has a reputation for complete honesty and fairness. Don'tcha hate people like that?! Boo … Hiss … KILL THE UMP! … Hah … just thought that one up. Hehe! Well enough preliminaries … The woman's up against the wall, and the starting pitcher is Hosea Canusee, and it looks like he's ready to go! Okay, sports fans, let's PLAY ROCKBALL!

WOMAN whimpers throughout, talking about how bad she is, how she deserves it and worse, even hell. ANNOUNCER gives each pitcher's name (possible "biblical" names with a twist: Hosea Canusee, Boaz' Babe Ruth; Tyre's Cobb; Zacher Jack, Philip Phanatic, Joshua Judgmental, Sarah Smashedher, Stephen Stonesher, Beulah Boulder, Boanerges Bomber, and so on). As each pitcher goes into the windup, JESUSUMP stops him with a question:

JESUSUMP

Wait! Have you ever sinned?

Each PITCHER admits he or she has sinned, ad libbing answers and excuses. After each excuse:

JESUSUMP

You're out of here!

PITCHERS show increasing frustration. After all the PITCHERS are ejected, the ANNOUNCER, very agitated, runs to the mound and picks up the ball, then tries to give the ball to JESUSUMP.

ANNOUNCER

(Yelling) Just a minute! I don't like this umpire business! You've ruined the game! I like to watch sinners get theirs. *(Pauses while he fumes)* Wait! I know! From what I hear, You've never done anything wrong. *(Taking the ball and stalking over to JESUSUMP)* You pitch!

JESUSUMP

(To ZEBEDEE) You're out of here! *(ZEBEDEE EXITS in a huff. JESUSUMP looks around.)* Is there no one left to throw stones? *(To WOMAN)* Go in peace, sin no more! *(To audience)* "There is no fear in love. Perfect love casts out fear."

ANNOUNCER

(Coming back on stage) Wow. How about that? It's a new game, now, folks! Looks like we're *all* sinners. We'd all have to be behind that home plate if it weren't for Jesus. But instead of leaving us losers, He makes us all winners! So long for now, sports fans. This is Zebedee MacGee, signing off.

Gracious Goodness, Great Tongues of Fire

Text: Acts 2:1–47

Level: Grade 3 and above

Participants: Narrator, Disciples (12, if possible, but at least 4), Crowd (a group larger than the Disciples), Scoffers (at least 2)

Props: A fan (the bigger the better); 12 red baseball caps (or 12 caps with the some kind of fire logo or symbol)

Sound: Stationary microphone for reader; lapel microphone for Peter and, if possible, for the other speakers.

Setting the Stage: *A simple set will do. The cast freezes whenever the NARRATOR speaks.*

NARRATOR

This is the story of the Church's birthday. It was the day when God gave His Holy Spirit to the disciples, 50 days after Easter. It goes something like this:

DISCIPLES are sitting together, reading loose sheets of paper, looking hot and fanning themselves. One sits up, suddenly.

DISCIPLE 1

Hey! Feel that wind?

DISCIPLE 2

It … it's amazing!

DISCIPLE 3

It feels great!

DISCIPLE 4

(Taking a huge, deep breath) I've never known such fresh air!

The fan is turned on, papers blow, the DISCIPLES get up, facing the wind. Then they sing or chant to the tune of "Great Balls of Fire:"

DISCIPLE 1

Just feel that breeze as it blows through your hair!

DISCIPLE 2

Just take a breath of this wonderful air!

DISCIPLE 1

Don't think it's odd,

DISCIPLE 2

It comes from God!

ALL DISCIPLES

Gracious goodness: I feel inspired!

NARRATOR

The wind was amazing, but it was just the beginning.

CROWD assembles (including SCOFFERS) around the DISCIPLES. They look around in wonder as if they also feel something wonderful. The DISCIPLES all put on their red caps at once.

DISCIPLE 3

(Pointing at another DISCIPLE) Look! Fire! *(Reaches to slap the flames out)*

DISCIPLE 4

(Pointing at different DISCIPLES in turn) Fire! Fire! Fire? Fire, but you're not burned?

All DISCIPLES ad lib as they point to one another's heads, reaching, waving their hands over the head of another DISCIPLE, seeing if they'll be burned.

DISCIPLE 3

(Sung) This makes no sense—I just cannot explain:
On ev'ry head some kinda fiery flame!

DISCIPLE 1

Don't think it's odd,

DISCIPLE 2

It comes from God!

ALL DISCIPLES

Gracious goodness: Great tongues of fire!

NARRATOR

Wind and fire—both were miracles to show the presence of the Holy Spirit. But there was still more to come!

DISCIPLE 4

Look at that crowd! They're from all over.

DISCIPLE 1

Let's tell them what happened to Jesus! Then they'll know why all this is happening too.

DISCIPLE 3

But they speak so many different languages.

DISCIPLE 2

Let's just do what we can!

DISCIPLES go toward CROWD and begin to speak—each one to a small group of two or three CROWD members. After a minute or two of ad libbing, perhaps using nonsense words to simulate the different languages, one group of three moves with their DISCIPLE to the front.

CROWD 1

(To CROWD 2) Hey, I can understand him!

CROWD 2

Me too!

CROWD 3

He's talking our language.

Other CROWD members exclaim similar things.

CROWD 1

(Sung) I can't believe what is filling my ear—
My mother tongue and it's perfectly clear!

DISCIPLE 1

Don't think it's odd,

DISCIPLE 2

It comes from God!

ALL DISCIPLES

Gracious goodness: great tongues of fire!

SCOFFERS now separate and move to the center. DISCIPLE 1 overhears their conversation.

SCOFFER 1

This is bogus! They're all just crazy!

SCOFFER 2

Yeah. I don't believe in miracles.

SCOFFER 1

If you ask me, they just went to night school and learned a new language.

SCOFFER 2

It's a conspiracy!

SCOFFER 1

Maybe they're just drunk!

SCOFFER 2

That's it!

SCOFFER 1

(Sung) We're pretty sure they just rattled their brains.

SCOFFER 2

Too much new wine drives a man insane.

SCOFFER 1 and 2

We think they're ill!
It's a cheap thrill.
But gracious goodness, we must inquire.

DISCIPLE 1

Wrong again, guys! It's a little early for wine. This isn't spirits ... It's *the* Spirit. The Holy Spirit.

NARRATOR

Peter and the other disciples told everyone who would listen to them that Jesus, who had died, was alive again. Some people couldn't believe the miracle that day, but others did—many others. The day that began when the Holy Spirit was given to the disciples in miracles of wind and fire and new languages ended with Him being given to thousands more who were baptized. You may not feel any wind, or see any tongues of fire, or hear new languages, but when you were baptized, God gave you His Spirit too. God promised Him that very day:

DISCIPLE 1

"Repent and be baptized, every one of you, in the name of Jesus Christ for the forgiveness of your sins. And you will receive the gift of the Holy Spirit. The promise is for you and your children and for all who are far off—for all whom the Lord our God will call" *(Acts 2:38–39).*

We're All Shook Up

~~~~~~~~~~~~~~~~~~~~~~~

Text: Matthew 28:1–4, Mark 1:1–8, Luke 24:13–16, 28–32, 36–37

Level: Grades 5–6 or mixed group including younger children

Participants: Reader, Chorus, 2–4 Priests, Servant, 2–4 Soldiers, Disciples (they can be the Chorus, including Peter, John, and 2 Emmaus Disciples), 3 Women, ("All" indicates that the Chorus joins in singing)

Props: Swords for soldiers; Bible costumes; round cardboard gravestone

Sound: A sound effect tape with sounds like an earthquake or thunderstorm, if possible. If not, the CHORUS will make a stomping noisy racket for the earthquake. Stationary microphone for Reader; lapel microphones, if possible, for other speakers.

Setting the Stage: *As the scene opens, the PRIESTS are standing upstage. A SERVANT is downstage, sitting. The READER goes to the microphone and begins.*

~~~~~~

READER

After the Sabbath, at dawn on the first day of the week, … there was a violent earthquake, for an angel of the Lord came down from heaven and, going to the tomb, rolled back the stone and sat on it. His appearance was like lightning, and his clothes were white as snow. The guards were so afraid of him that they shook and became like dead men *(Matthew 28:1–4).*

Play the sound effect tape or have the CHORUS off to the side stomp and shake and make loud rumbling noises. The PRIESTS shake a little, then look at one another and shrug. After a pause, they hear distant noises. Then the SOLDIERS come running up noisily from the center aisle and stop at the SERVANT, shaking nervously, hanging onto each other in a group. They look behind them like they've seen a ghost. They continue to shake throughout their lines. The SERVANT brings them to the PRIESTS.

SERVANT

The guards from the grave of Jesus are here.

PRIEST 1

(Noticing the shaking) What's wrong with you? You look like you've seen a ghost.

The SOLDIERS nudge each other back and forth, still clinging and shaking, shaking their heads both yes and no until one steps forward.

SOLDIER 1

We have good news and bad news.

PRIEST 2

What's the good news?

SOLDIER 2

Nobody stole His body.

PRIEST 1

Good! So, what's the bad news?

The SOLDIERS nudge each other back and forth again.

SOLDIER 1

(*Mumbling, still looking all around*) He's not there.

PRIEST 1

What?

SOLDIER 1

(*A little louder, still petrified*) He's not there.

PRIEST 1

What!?

The following lines are sung to the tune of "I'm All Shook Up."

SOLDIER 1

A well a help me, please, somethin's wrong with me.
I'm shakin' like a leaf on a willow tree.
My friends are all crazy, just as scared as me.

SOLDIERS

Our eyes are blurry from the strangest sight
We were guardin' the grave while it's dark as night
When there's a bang and roar and a blast of light.
He's alive!

ALL

We're all shook up, u-uh-huh, yeah, oh yeah!

PRIESTS

Now we've heard everything! Get out of here *(PRIESTS chase SOLDIERS offstage.)*

Scene 2: *The DISCIPLES are standing in a group.*

READER

When the Sabbath was over, Mary Magdalene, Mary the mother of James, and Salome bought spices so that they might go to anoint Jesus' body. Very early on the first day of the week, just after sunrise, they were on their way to the tomb and they asked each other, "Who will roll the stone away from the entrance of the tomb?" But when they looked up, they saw that the stone, which was very large, had been rolled away. As they entered the tomb, they saw a young man dressed in a white robe sitting on the right side, and they were alarmed. "Don't be alarmed," he said. "You are looking for Jesus the Nazarene, who was crucified. He has risen! He is not here. See the place where they laid Him. But go, tell His disciples and Peter, 'He is going ahead of you into Galilee. There you will see Him, just as He told you.'" Trembling and bewildered, the women went out and fled from the tomb. They said nothing to anyone, because they were afraid *(Mark 16:1–8).*

The WOMEN come running up the aisle to the DISCIPLES, shaking and hanging onto one another, looking frightened but also excited. They continue to shake throughout their lines.

DISCIPLE 1

What's wrong? You look like you saw a ghost!

The WOMEN shake their heads no as they cling to one another.

WOMAN 1

No ... no ghost. An earthquake!

WOMAN 2

No ... no ghost. An angel!

WOMAN 3

No ... no ghost. Jesus!

WOMAN 1

(Sung) A well a help me, please, somethin's wrong with me.
I'm shakin' like a leaf on a willow tree.
My friends are all crazy, just as scared as me.

WOMEN

He's alive!
We're all shook up, u-uh-huh, yeah, oh yeah!
We're were walkin' to the grave in the early dawn—
See the grave wide open 'cause the stone is gone

There's an angel standin' right there on the lawn,
(Shouting) He's alive!

ALL

We're all shook up, u-uh-huh, yeah, oh yeah!

PETER and JOHN run out and the other DISCIPLES freeze.

READER

Now that same day two of them were going to the village called Emmaus, about seven miles from Jerusalem. They were talking with each other about everything that had happened. As they talked and discussed these things with each other, Jesus Himself came up and walked along with them; but they were kept from recognizing Him. As they approached the village to which they were going, Jesus acted as if He were going farther. But they urged Him strongly, "Stay with us, for it is nearly evening; the day is almost over." So He went in to stay with them. When He was at the table with them, He took bread, gave thanks, broke it, and began to give it to them. Then their eyes were opened and they recognized Him, and He disappeared from their sight. They asked each other, "Were not our hearts burning within us while He talked with us on the road and opened the Scriptures to us?" *(Luke 24:13–16, 28–32).*

Scene 3: *The EMMAUS DISCIPLES hurry down the center aisle, shaking and excited. They join the other DISCIPLES.*

EMMAUS 1

You'll never believe it!

EMMAUS 2

It's amazing!

EMMAUS 1

A well a help me, please, somethin's wrong with me.
I'm shakin' like a leaf on a willow tree.
My friends are all crazy, just as scared as me.

BOTH

He's alive!
We're all shook up, u-uh-huh, yeah, oh yeah!
We met the Lord Jesus on the road today.
He opened our eyes when we heard Him say,
"The Savior had to suffer before Glory Day!"
(Shouting) He's alive!

ALL

We're all shook up, u-uh-huh, yeah, oh yeah!

READER

While they were still talking about this, Jesus Himself stood among them and said to them, "Peace be with you." They were startled and frightened, thinking they saw a ghost *(Luke 24:36–37)*.

JESUS

Peace be with you.

The DISCIPLES are frightened, shaking and clinging. JESUS sings as He EXITS, followed by the DISCIPLES. They sing their final line just before they EXIT.

JESUS

You're scared to death, like you've seen a ghost.
Touch Me and see, and then diagnose:
I'm no longer dead! I'm not comatose!
I'm alive!

ALL

(Pointing to Jesus) Now everyone *look*! He's alive! Oh ... yeah!

All actors EXIT.

READER

Then He opened their minds so they could understand the Scriptures. He told them, "This is what is written: The Christ will suffer and rise from the dead on the third day, and repentance and forgiveness of sins will be preached in His name to all nations" *(Luke 24:45–47)*.

He's So Vain

〰〰〰〰〰〰〰〰

Text: Matthew 19:16–26

Level: Grades 3 and above

Participants: Narrator, Rich Young Man, Chorus, Jesus

Props: Suit and tie for Rich Young Man (the corporate look); wallet; lots of play money

Sound: Stationary microphone for Reader; lapel microphones, if possible, for other speakers.

Setting the Stage: *A simple set will do.*

〰〰〰〰〰〰〰〰〰〰〰〰〰〰〰〰〰〰

NARRATOR

One day, while Jesus was teaching people about God's kingdom, a very wealthy and successful young man came up to Him to ask Him a question.

MAN

Teacher, what good thing must I do to get eternal life?

JESUS

Why do you ask Me about what is good? There is only One who is good. If you want to enter life, obey the commandments.

MAN

Which ones?

JESUS

Do not murder, do not commit adultery, do not steal, do not give false testimony, honor your father and mother, and love your neighbor as yourself.

MAN

All these I have kept.

CHORUS

(Sung to the tune of "You're So Vain" by Carly Simon)
He's so vain, we wrote this silly song about him.
He's so vain, we wrote this silly song all about him, 'bout him, 'bout him.

136

MAN

Well, I'm rich and I am powerful, my friends all think I'm cool.
I work for a prestigious firm, 'cause I went to the finest school.
I do what I should all the time and when I don't it's 'cause
I have an excuse or a good explanation, a good explanation.

CHORUS

See?
He's so vain, we wrote this silly song all about him.
He's so vain, we wrote this silly song all about him, 'bout him, 'bout him.

MAN

I just always do the right things, and I do them oh so well!
But I have this nagging feeling that I'm still not safe from hell.
So tell me, will You, Rabbi man, and I'll do what I can
To make it quite sure that I'll be there in heaven, I'll be there in heaven.

CHORUS

See?
He's so vain, we wrote this silly song all about him.
He's so vain, we wrote this silly song all about him, 'bout him, 'bout him.

Actors freeze.

NARRATOR

Now, what should Jesus do? This wealthy young man really believes that he's done everything that God would ever want him to do, and that he's never done anything wrong. Of course, all around him are needy people that he hasn't helped, hungry people he didn't feed, strangers that he ignored, sick people he hasn't helped, naked people while he wears the finest clothes, and people in prisons that he hasn't visited.

MAN

What do I still lack?

JESUS

If you want to be perfect, go, sell your possessions and give to the poor, and you will have treasure in heaven. Then come, follow Me.

The RICH YOUNG MAN looks stunned, takes out his wallet and brings out a fistful of money, looking at it and then at JESUS. After a long pause, he puts the money back in his wallet, hangs his head in sorrow, and EXITS, muttering to himself.

NARRATOR

When the young man heard this, he went away sad, because he had great wealth.

JESUS

(To the CHORUS) I tell you the truth, it is hard for a rich man to enter the kingdom of heaven. Again I tell you, it is easier for a camel to go through the eye of a needle than for a rich man to enter the kingdom of God.

CHORUS

Then who can be saved?

JESUS

For people this is impossible, but with God, all things are possible.

NARRATOR

For God so loved the world that He gave His one and only Son, that whoever believes in Him shall not perish but have eternal life *(John 3:16)*.

CHORUS

It's by grace, the only way we'll make it to heaven, it's by grace,
The only way we'll make it to heaven, heaven, heaven.
When we think we're better than anything, better than fresh, sliced bread,
We need someone somewhere to clue us in, and tell us it's all in our head.
If Jesus hadn't come along, we'd all end up all wrong.
So hopelessly lost and without any chances, without any chances.
But it's by grace, that all of us can make it to heaven, it's by grace,
The only way we'll make it to heaven, heaven, heaven.
(Shouting) Yes!

The Angels' Locker Room: A Christmas Play

Text: Luke 1:1–2:32

Level: Primary with adult help

Participants: God, Michael, Gabriel, Angels (any number)

Props: Football helmets; papers wings for angels; T-shirts for God, Michael, and Gabriel; headphones for God

Sound: Lapel microphone for God, Michael, and Gabriel

Setting the Stage: *ANGELS are in uniform with football helmets and wings. The wings have numbers. GOD wears headphones like a football coach and a big sign front and back saying "Head Coach." MICHAEL and GABRIEL wear T-shirts that say "Assistant."*

GOD

Okay, team. It's the big event! The big show! It's time to beat the devil once and for all. He's been tearing My people up down there! *(ANGELS hang their heads.)* Aw, no, I'm not criticizing. You guys have done a good job, protecting in all kinds of ways. But the devil is *so* tough. But, don't worry 'cause we're gonna get it done now! I've planned the work, and now it's time to work the plan!

Several ANGELS begin shouting.

ANGEL 1

Let us at 'em!

ANGEL 2

We can beat them on the ground—nobody has moves like an angel!

ANGEL 3

Wait till they see our passing game. Remember the Passover that beat Egypt?

ANGELS shout and clamor.

GOD

Calm down, calm down. Ya' gotta listen. That's not the way to beat the devil. I know you guys wiped out Sodom and Gomorrah, right? *(ANGELS nod their heads and raise their fists, shouting and boasting after each question, getting louder and more raucous each time.)* And you wiped out Pharoah, right? ... And you wiped out Sennacherib, right? ... and Babylon? ... and the Medes and Persians? ... and the Greeks? *(Pause)* But that didn't stop the devil, did it?

Dead silence—all the ANGELS hang their heads.

GOD

Stop feelin' bad. You did your job. But that's not how you beat the devil and his guys.

MICHAEL

So, how we gonna do it, God?

GOD

Alright, I need Gabe. C'mere. Here's what you do on this play: Head straight down, cut right to Jerusalem, and tell Zechariah his wife, Elizabeth, is gonna have a boy.

GABRIEL

Elizabeth? She's old.

ANGELS

Old? Old people are wimpy!

GOD

Their kid will set things up for the big play against Satan. Okay? Then, after that, cut left to touch down in Galilee.

GABRIEL

Touchdown? Did you say touchdown? *(GABRIEL raises both arms and does touchdown dance.)* He scores!

GOD

(Shaking His head) When you get to Galilee, find Mary and stick with her. She's your assignment.

GABRIEL

Whoa, wait. A girl?

GOD

Yeah. She's just right.

BOY ANGELS

A girl? Girls are wimpy!

140

GOD

Yeah, a girl! A boy couldn't do it.

GIRL ANGELS

Yeah! Do what?

GOD

Have a baby.

ANGELS

A baby? Babies are wimpy!

GOD

The baby's gonna be a new king!

GABRIEL

Alright! Kings are cool! Off to Jerusalem. Can't wait to see the palace … *(In football stance)* Down, set!

GOD

He's not going to be born in a palace. Nope! The plan is He's born in a stable.

MICHAEL

A stable? With sheep and stuff?

ANGELS

Sheep? Sheep are wimpy!

GOD

It's a stable! In Bethlehem.

ANGELS

Bethlehem? Bethlehem's wimpy!

GOD

I know. It's a dinky little town, and it's far away from Galilee. That's why Gabriel's going. First he tells them what I'm doing, then he protects Mary and her husband all the way.

MICHAEL

Good. So the kid's dad is going?

GOD

Nope, he's just Joseph, Mary's husband, but not the Baby's dad. I'll be the kid's dad.

ANGELS

WHAAAAT?

MICHAEL

You're sending your own *SuperSon* to be ... HUMAN?

ANGELS

Human? Human's are wimpy!

MICHAEL

The devil will kill Him!

GABRIEL

Destroy Him!

ANGELS

Wipe Him out!

GOD

Don't get My plan? Good! If you don't get it, Satan won't either. He'll see how little My Son is, and think that makes Him too wimpy and weak. He won't figure out that this weak little Baby's gonna take away all his devilish power—until it's too late! Remember! That little Baby's still gonna be *My* Son.

ANGELS

(Cheering and clapping) Alright, God! Great plan!

GOD

Okay, team, huddle up. *(Entire group assembles in huddle with their hands stacked on GOD'S.)* 1-2-3. Angels ho! Down you go! Kick them demons down the hole! Go angels! Go angels!

ANGELS

Go, Go, Go, Go, GO!

GOD

Let's sing our fight song!

ANGELS

(Sung to the tune of "Glory, Glory, Hallelujah")
Glory, glory, hallelujah!
The Baby's gonna sock it to the
Devil, he won't know what hit 'im
His time is almost gone!

GOD

Hold on, angels! Don't lose focus. It may feel great to beat the devil, but we're doing it all for them *(pointing to audience)* so we can *all* be together here in heaven. Now, go team, go team, go, go, go! *(Everyone scatters, like a football team breaking huddle.)*

The Temptations

Text: Matthew 4:1–11, Luke 4:1–13

Level: Grades 4–6

Participants: Reader, 2 Angel Narrators, Jesus, Demon Chorus (including two speakers), Satan

Props: Crushed brown paper bags to look like larger stones; several stones that are about the size of a loaf of bread; footlocker, chest, or box for Satan's props; either a slide projector with a beautiful panoramic slide or large travel brochures; a large stepladder with a large cardboard cross affixed to the side that will face the audience; costumes that indicate demons and angels (red and white shirts will do); picnic basket or lunch box

Sound: Stationary microphone for Reader; lapel microphones, if possible, for other speakers.

Setting the Stage: *The set should have the stones scattered around. If a projector is used, the screen should be upstage. JESUS is centerstage, lying down or leaning against a bigger stone, looking exhausted. The ANGELS are to one side, looking worried. SATAN and his CHORUS enter from the other side. JESUS shows that He hears the DEMONS and SATAN, but when the ANGELS speak, JESUS gives no indication that He hears.*

READER

Jesus, full of the Holy Spirit, returned from the Jordan and was led by the Spirit in the desert, where for forty days He was tempted by the devil. He ate nothing during those days, and at the end of them He was hungry *(Luke 4:1–2)*.

ANGEL 1

Forty days all alone! Forty days in the desert! Forty days without eating!

ANGEL 2

Imagine how weak and hungry He felt after all that time.

JESUS

I'm so hungry!

READER

The tempter came to Him and said, "If You are the Son of God, tell these stones to become bread" *(Matthew 4:3).*

ANGEL 1

Poor Jesus! *(Yelling at SATAN)* Ya' big meanie!

ANGEL 2

Wouldn't you know it? Just when you're weakest, along comes the devil!

SATAN ENTERS, swaggering. DEMONS ENTER, scuffling and scurrying about.

SATAN

So You're the Son of God? Hmmm. *(JESUS sits up, then stands, but still looks weak.)*

DEMON 1

But You're hungry?

DEMON 2

There's nothing like bread when you're starving!

SATAN

God can do anything He wants. He made the world just by speaking. If You're His Son, let's see You do it, Jesus. Just make some bread. *(Picking up a stone and showing it to JESUS)* Use this stone and make some bread!

DEMON 1

Yeah, and eat.

DEMON 2

(DEMONS all pick up stones.) Make enough for everybody!

SATAN

Think of how many people You could feed with all these rocks. Come on! It wouldn't be selfish—You'd be practicing. *(Waving the stone temptingly in front of JESUS)* And You wouldn't be hungry!

DEMONS

(Singing to the tune of "I Can Give You the World" from Disney's Aladdin. *DEMONS form a semicircle behind JESUS, singing to Him.)*
Feed yourself, feed the world,
Give them food. Give them money.
Make some bread for the hungry.
Give them all they want to eat.

SATAN

Begin right now. You're hungry, make this stone a roll.
If you are God's own Son, it's good as done,
Why worry? Bread could not affect Your soul.

ANGEL 1

Don't trust him, Jesus. Isn't he sneaky?

ANGEL 2

Jesus is starving hungry, and the devil wants Him to use His power for Himself, like it was magic or something.

ANGEL 1

Jesus *could* make rocks into bread if He wanted to.

ANGEL 2

But then who would work anymore? And who would share what they have with others?

ANGEL 1

It's too tempting. I know He'll do it! Oh no!

ANGEL 2

Sshhhhh.

READER

Jesus said:

JESUS

It is written: "Man does not live on bread alone, but on every word that comes from the mouth of God."

ANGEL 1

Alright Jesus! I'm glad that's over! Why don't we give Him something to eat now?

ANGEL 2

Wait, it's not over yet.

The DEMONS bring out a large stepladder and set it up. SATAN leads JESUS to the ladder and has Him climb to the top while SATAN stands beneath it.

READER

Then the devil took Jesus to the holy city and had Him stand on the highest point of the temple. "If You are the Son of God," he said, "throw Yourself down. For it is written: 'He will command His angels concerning You, and they will lift You up in their hands, so that You will not strike Your foot against a stone' " *(Matthew 4:5–6).*

SATAN

Look at those crowds down there. They're just waiting for a leader.

DEMON 1

Somebody impressive!

DEMON 2

(Pointing to SATAN) Like him!

SATAN

Or, like You, if You do the right thing! *(Pauses, thinking)* If You're God's Son, I'm sure You can do something to attract their attention.

DEMON 1

Something to wow the crowd.

DEMON 2

And prove You're God!

ANGEL 1

He *is* God, and you know it!

ANGEL 2

Shhh. Just watch.

SATAN

I've got it! Picture this, Jesus: You do a huge swan dive, right off the top. Everyone gasps.

DEMONS

(Gasping in fake amazement) Ooooohhhhhhhhhh!!

SATAN

(Mimicking a baseball outfielder making a catch) But the angels catch You! Proving to You—and the crowd—that You really are God's Son!

DEMON 1

Yeah! *(DEMONS cheer.)*

DEMON 2

(To JESUS, pointing to SATAN) Do what he says ... he's smart!

DEMONS

(Pointing to SATAN and singing)
He impresses the world!
Makes them wild and excited

Takes their love unrequited
That's their problem, don't you see?

SATAN

Just take the dive. His angels will keep You alive
They'll come and lift You up, like powder puffs,
Why worry? Show the crowds Your awesome stuff.

JESUS looks down, contemplatively.

ANGEL 1

Don't jump! *(Covering his eyes)* He's gonna jump! I know He's gonna jump!

ANGEL 2

The crowd would be impressed if He jumped. And He could catch Himself—He doesn't need us. But I don't think that's the Father's way.

SATAN

Remember, the Bible says: "He will command His angels concerning You, and they will lift You up in their hands, so that You will not strike Your foot against a stone."

READER

But Jesus said:

JESUS

It also says, "Do not put the Lord your God to the test" *(Luke 4:12)*.

The DEMONS carry the ladder away. If a projector is used, project the panoramic slide, otherwise, have SATAN open up the travel brochure and show it to JESUS.

READER

Again, the devil took Him to a very high mountain and showed Him all the kingdoms of the world and their splendor. "All this I will give You," he said, "if You will bow down and worship me" *(Matthew 4:8–9)*.

ANGEL 1

Wow, look at that scenery!

ANGEL 2

It would be wonderful to rule everything.

SATAN

Now, please remember that I can influence everybody on earth, one way or another. It can all be Yours. If You listen to me, all the rulers will follow You and so will all the people. Think about it.

DEMON 1

Money!

DEMON 2

Power!

SATAN

Think of the rich cities! All the money in all the banks! All the armies that will do whatever You say! All the people who will run to do Your bidding!

DEMON 1

He can make You famous!

DEMON 2

He can give You the world!

DEMONS

(Gathering around JESUS and singing)
Let him give You the world!
Coast to coast—see the glitter
Here's Your chance, don't You fritter
All the joys of pow'r away.

SATAN

A whole new world!
It's Yours I'll give it all to You.
Just get down on Your knees and worship me.
It's mine, my world is waiting here for You.

ANGEL 1

Oh, that's tempting! *(Covering his eyes)* He's gonna do it!

ANGEL 2

All that power, just waiting for Him.

SATAN

What do You think, Jesus? I think You'd be a great ruler. Better than any of the other ones. *(Pushing gently on JESUS' shoulders)* Just show me a little respect ... *(Pushing harder)* Show me that You're with me. *(Pushing as hard as he can)* Just ... bow ... DOWN!

READER

But Jesus said,

JESUS

(Removing SATAN'S hands, as if they are nothing) Away from Me, Satan! For it is written: "Worship the Lord your God, and serve Him only" *(Matthew 4:10).*

SATAN/DEMONS

(As JESUS speaks, SATAN and the DEMONS EXIT, walking backward as if they are blown by a strong wind, screaming loudly and ad libbing complaints until they are out of sight.) Aaaahhhhh! I hate You! Who needs You? Wimp! Loser! Fool! Blockhead! Idiot!

ANGEL 1

Yeah, Jesus! I knew You'd do it! Never doubted You for a minute!

ANGEL 2

C'mon! Now we get to help Him. Bring that food! *(ANGEL 1 grabs the picnic basket. Both rush out to JESUS and EXIT with Him, one on either side.)*

READER

Then the devil left Him, and angels came and attended Him *(Matthew 4:11).*

Yakety Yak: He Won't Talk Back

***

Text: Isaiah 53:3–7, Matthew 27:11–14

Level: Grades 3–6

Participants: Reader, Pilate, Priests, Herod, Mob, Soldiers, Jesus

Props: T-shirts and markers; purple robe (perhaps a Lenten chasuble); crown of thorns; cross with a box or stand in front so Jesus can stand on it with His arms stretched out to the side

Sounds: Stationary microphone for Reader, lapel microphones, if possible, for other speakers.

Setting the Stage: *A simple set will do. The characters wear T-shirts with signs that identify the characters, except for JESUS, who is dressed plainly. The cross is upstage, center. Everyone except JESUS sings the last stanza of the song, looking at the audience with surprise and shrugging their shoulders. The PRIESTS join the MOB for the MOB'S lines.*

***

READER

When He was accused by the chief priests and the elders, He gave no answer. Then Pilate asked Him, "Don't You hear the testimony they are bringing against You?" But Jesus made no reply, not even to a single charge—to the great amazement of the governor *(Matthew 27:12–14)*.

PILATE

(Sung to the tune of "Yakety Yak!")
Here is your chance to have Your say.
Good luck don't come along each day.
C'mon give me the exposé.
I am Your only getaway!

ALL

(Sung) Yakety Yak! *(Spoken)* He won't talk back!

PILATE

(To himself) What's with Him? Why won't He defend Himself? Everybody else is talking around here. Why won't He?

PRIESTS

This guy is nothing but trouble! We already had a trial and we sentenced Him to death. *(Sung)*
This man is spreadin' blasphemy!
Don't you dare give Him amnesty.
He threatens Caesar's harmony.
Go take Him out to Calvary.

ALL

(Sung) Yakety Yak! *(Spoken)* He won't talk back!

PILATE

(To himself, thinking) I don't like this. I think this guy's an idiot for not talking, but I can't put Him to death for that. This is gonna be trouble.

PRIESTS

Well? What are you going to do with this Galilean?

PILATE

(Brightening) Galilean? Did you say "Galilean?" I'll hand Him over to Herod, the Tetrarch of Galilee! *(Off to the side, cupping his hands to yell in a singsong)* Oh, Her—od, come here!

HEROD

(ENTERS from the side. JESUS is led to him by the soldiers.) Jesus? Oh boy! *(To himself)* I've been wanting to see this guy do one of His miracles. I can't wait. Lemme see. One miracle … no two miracles and I let Him go. *(Sung)*
You listen good now, Pontius Pi!
It's time to kill Him—*(shouted)* Crucify!
He had His chances to reply.
He wouldn't talk—He's gotta die.

ALL

(Sung) Yakety Yak! *(Spoken)* He won't talk back!

(HEROD pauses, staring angrily at JESUS with his hands on his hips, then stalks to the side.)

HEROD

All right! Forget You! Pilate, you take Him!

PILATE

(Reluctantly) Ok—ay. *(Pauses, then a lightbulb)* I have it! Look, here's the choice: I either let this guy go, or that blood-thirsty, hideous, ax-murdering criminal Barabbas! Okay?

MOB

Barabbas! *(Sung)*
This is your chance to strut Your stuff.
One miracle will be enough.
Just heal somebody off-the-cuff.
That won't be hard and it ain't tough!

ALL

Yakety Yak! *(Spoken)* He won't talk back.

PILATE

(To himself) Uh oh! Now what? ... Got it! I'll let the soldiers have fun with Him. Then He'll start talking and the crowd will feel sorry and let Him go. *(To the SOLDIERS)* Let Him have it!

SOLDIERS

(Rubbing their hands gleefully) You've had it now!

The SOLDIERS put the robe and the crown on JESUS, then pretend to hit Him, knock Him down, and kick Him. Then they stand around Him in a circle, looking puzzled.

SOLDIERS

(Sung) We made Him wear that thorny crown.
We put on Him that purple gown.
We beat Him up and beat Him down.
But He just never made a sound.

ALL

Yakety Yak! *(Spoken)* He won't talk back.

PILATE

Nothing works with You! This is Your last chance: *(Sung)*
You've got one minute to explain.
This is Your chance to miss the pain.
I am the one who can restrain
These angry people. Use Your brain!

ALL

Yakety Yak! *(Spoken incredulously)* He won't talk back?

PILATE

(To JESUS) Well? Well? WELL??

The SOLDIERS, followed by the MOB, take JESUS back to the cross and have Him stand on the box with His arms outstretched. They mime nailing Him to the cross, then they stand back.

MOB

Some king! Fake! Failure! Loser! Nyah, Nyah!

SOLDIERS

Here, King, You want a drink?

MOB

C'mon. We thought You worked miracles. Save somebody now! Like Yourself! *(Sung)* For someone with Your following,
Your weakness is astonishing,
Just jump on down if You're the king.
We'll take Your word on everything.

ALL

Yakety Yak! *(Spoken)* He won't talk back.

MOB

What a loser!

SOLDIERS

What a loser!

ALL

What a LOSER!

SOLDIERS

(Peering up at the cross) A dead loser! *(Sung)*
We did the job just like they said.
When Pilate gave the go-ahead,
We nailed Him up, His arms outspread.
Our job is done 'cause now He's dead.

ALL

Yakety Yak! *(Spoken)* He won't talk back.

JESUS is taken down from the cross and laid down. Everyone gathers around, looking down at Him.

ALL

(Loudly) He won't talk back!

All the characters freeze as READER concludes.

READER

He was despised and rejected by men, a man of sorrows, and familiar with suffering. Like one from whom men hide their faces He was despised, and we esteemed Him not.

Surely He took up our infirmities and carried our sorrows, yet we considered Him stricken by God, smitten by Him, and afflicted. But He was pierced for our transgressions, He was crushed for our iniquities; the punishment that brought us peace was upon Him, and by His wounds we are healed. We all, like sheep, have gone astray, each of us has turned to his own way; and the LORD has laid on Him the iniquity of us all. He was oppressed and afflicted, yet He did not open His mouth; He was led like a lamb to the slaughter, and as a sheep before her shearers is silent, so He did not open His mouth *(Isaiah 53:3–7)*.

Be My Guest

Text: Luke 14:15–24, Matthew 22:2–14

Level: A mixed age group—an older child who can sing should play the King, younger children can play the other parts

Participants: Reader, King, Servants (4 or more), Friends (a group of 3 or more), and the Needy (4 or more, sitting with the audience)

Props: Crown; kingly garments (colorful robes that look expensive); ripped and dirty garments; a wheelchair (or walker); dark glasses; a cane

Sound: Stationary microphone for Reader; lapel microphones, if possible, for other speakers.

Setting the Stage: *The KING is upstage, elevated if possible. The table is covered with bowls and goblets, etc. The KING wears a crown and garments that suggest wealth and importance. Downstage left are the FRIENDS, looking self-important and crabby.*

READER

A reading from Luke, chapter 14, beginning with verse 16: "A certain man was preparing a great banquet and invited many guests. At the time of the banquet he sent his servant to tell those who had been invited, 'Come, for everything is now ready.' "

SERVANTS

Everything is ready for your son's wedding.

KING

Wonderful! Now I can call my friends!

The KING moves forward with hands to his mouth as if he is calling the FRIENDS. The SERVANTS and KING dance while the KING sings.

KING

(Sung to the tune of "Be Our Guest" from Disney's Beauty and the Beast.*)*
Be my guest! Be my guest! The finest food you will ingest
My son's wedding soon is starting. Can't you see? It's manifest.
Join your friends! Share my joy at the marriage of my boy.
If you've any aspiration to take part in my salvation

Come and dance! Come and sing! It's the marriage of the king.

SERVANTS

(Sung) And there's nothing here that's any less than best.

KING

(Sung) Your wedding clothes are all you need to bring; and then
You'll be my guest, yes, my guest! Be my guest!
(Looking puzzled, speaking) Maybe they didn't hear me. Go and invite them to come and celebrate with us. We have the finest of everything all ready for them! I have spared no expense for my wonderful son's wedding!

READER

"But [the invited guests] all alike began to make excuses. The first said, 'I have bought a field, and I must go and see it. Please excuse me.' Another said, 'I have just bought five yoke of oxen, and I'm on my way to try them out. Please excuse me.' Still another said, 'I just got married, so I cannot come.' "

One SERVANT goes to the FRIENDS, who turn their backs on him. Only when, one by one, each FRIEND is tapped on the shoulder does the FRIEND turn and acknowledge the SERVANT.

SERVANT

(To FRIEND 1) It's time for the wedding.

FRIEND 1

I'm too busy! (FRIEND 1 walks to the other side of the stage with head held high, looking self-important.)

SERVANT

(To FRIEND 2) It's time for the wedding.

FRIEND 2

I'm much too busy! (FRIEND 2 walks to the other side of the stage with head held high, looking self-important.)

SERVANT

(To FRIEND 3) It's time for the wedding.

FRIEND 3

I'm far too busy! (FRIEND 3 walks to the other side of the stage with head held high, looking self-important. The FRIENDS gather together to sing.)

FRIENDS

(Sung) We protest! We suggest his wedding feast is second-best
To the things we'd rather do instead—the heck with his request!

We must work, we must play and we'll do it our own way.
We don't want his celebration and forget his dumb salvation!
Don't you see, we must be, about our own priorities?
All that good stuff you like—well—we just detest.
Go on and celebrate without us, we don't care
To be your guests. We reject your request!

The FRIENDS turn in a huff and stomp off the stage. The SERVANT returns to the KING.

READER

So the servant came back and reported this to his master.

SERVANT

They don't want to come.

KING

(Incredulously) What? They won't celebrate with my own dear son? *(Angrily)* Then we will celebrate without them! This is what I want you to do! *(Whispers to SERVANTS)*

READER

[The master said:] "Go out at once into the streets and lanes of the town and bring in the poor, the crippled, the blind, and the lame."

The SERVANTS walk out toward the audience.

SERVANTS

(Sung) Be his guest! Be his guest! The finest food you will ingest.
His son's wedding soon is starting. Can't you see? It's manifest.
Join your friends! Share his joy, at the marriage of his boy.
If you've any aspiration to take part in his salvation
Come and dance! Come and sing! It's the marriage of the king
And there's nothing here that's any less than best.
Your wedding clothes are all you need to bring; and then
You'll be his guest, yes, his guest! Be his guest!

Individual SERVANTS help the NEEDY forward: one dressed in rags, one in the wheelchair or using the walker, one in dark glasses, walking like a blind person, and one with the cane.

READER

" 'Sir,' the servant said, 'what you ordered has been done, but there is still room.' Then the master told his servant, 'Go out to the roads and country lanes, and make them come in, so that my house will be full. I tell you, not one of those who were invited will get a taste of my banquet' " *(Luke 14:22–24).*

SERVANTS go back out to the audience. This last stanza is sung directly to the audience.

KING

(Sung) Be my guest! Be my guest! The finest food you will ingest.
My son's wedding soon is starting. Can't you see? It's manifest.

SERVANTS

(Sung) Be his friend! Share his joy, at the marriage of his boy.
If you've any aspiration to take part in his salvation
Come and dance! Come and sing! It's the marriage of the king

KING

(Sung) And there's nothing here that's any less than best.

SERVANTS

(Sung) Your wedding clothes are all you need to bring; and then
You'll be his guest,

KING

(Sung) Yes, my guest!

SERVANTS

(Sung) Be his guest!

Index